On the Sanctity of Human Life:

Considerations Regarding Life and End-of-Life Issues

Peter F. Connell

Foreword by

Philip Harrelson

On the Sanctity of Human Life:

Considerations Regarding Life and End-of-Life Issues

ଔ

A publication of

APOSTOLIC TRUTH
PUBLICATIONS
A Ministry of
Cornerstone Pentecostal Church
PO Box 383
Oakley, California 94561

Available from Amazon.com and other online stores

DEDICATION

To my mother, Irene Connell. Events surrounding her final moments served as a significant motivation for writing this book.

ACKNOWLEDGEMENTS

A great many thanks to those who, following my initial presentation of this subject as a paper in January 2012, encouraged me to expand upon the subject, and to publish it more broadly. Included in that number were Jerry and Roffie Ensey, Philip Harrelson, Steve Waldron, Ben Weeks and William Davis.

I'd like to express additional heartfelt thanks to those who helped me with suggestions, edits or in some other way contributed to the content of this book—some of whom are already mentioned above. These include Jerry Ensey, Dennis Garza, Nathan Dudley, Kevin Nix, David Bernard, Kelly Nix, Tim Cormier, Scott Hillman and my neighbor, John Ricafort. Thanks to some additional men who reviewed the book and kindly forwarded an endorsement. These include James Groce, Tim Copeland, Tim Lackey and Derrald Hilderbrand.

Thanks to Ryan Herras for helping me finalize the cover; and to my brother-in-law, John Contino, for helping me navigate those word processing functions quite beyond my technical capacity.

Very special thanks go to Philip Harrelson who gave me invaluable insight from the unique perspective of a seasoned pastor and one who has been involved as a healthcare professional for many years. Your sage advice surely made this a much better book that it would have otherwise been. You have honored me by writing the Foreword.

Table of Contents

FOREWORD

The book you hold in your hands (or are reading from an electronic device) is very important. It deals with several very emotional issues, such as end-of-life decisions, abortion, stem cell research and other things that are encroaching into even the most sheltered Apostolic environments. Great change in the world of advancing technology—particularly in medicine—has brought us to a place that is very similar to the Babylonian environment Daniel and his brethren found themselves in centuries ago. Because of this, Apostolics are being pushed to define their biblical worldview, which is a very profitable endeavor. With biblical illiteracy on the rise in America (and, sadly, even among some Apostolics), this work that Brother Connell has given us is of critical importance to that effort.

I read this book with an effort to lean toward my primary calling as an Apostolic minister, but I have also been a medical professional for more than 30 years. Honestly speaking, this book pushed me to the edge – not because the book is wrong, but because it unlocked gates for me to see for myself the humanistic and secular mindset that is foisting itself upon medicine and what should be considered appropriate medical practice in our nation. The Deep South, where I pastor and work, has not been as drastically affected as some other locations in the country, but there is still a very real spiritual onslaught about which we must educate ourselves.

Every Apostolic who is involved in healthcare needs to read this book carefully. However, it is not just for those in the field of medicine; it is vitally important for good pastors and saints who increasingly find themselves swimming against the atheistic stream of thought that is prevalent in America. I would encourage you to read it through once and then go back and thoughtfully read it again, giving deep consideration to what Brother Connell has shared with us as a concerned fellow pastor and brother in the Lord.

Philip Harrelson
Pastor, The Pentecostals of Dothan
Dothan, Alabama

PREFACE

In January of 2012 we were, it seemed, turning a corner in America. The healthcare package known as the Patient Protection and Affordable Care Act (hereinafter, ObamaCare), denied by voters and our elected representatives in Congress, was made possible by an (unconstitutional) act of judicial fiat led by U.S. Supreme Court Justice, John Roberts—and was just starting to be implemented. Financial, political and moral conflicts were serving to blur lines at an ever-increasing rate—lines of what was ethically and morally acceptable and what was not.

Granted, these lines had been the subject of attack long before the time of the Obama presidency; yet it was the events which were then before us, together with my personal experience and study, that compelled me to write on this subject in particular at that time. I saw a great need to address the issue at hand, and still see the need, so I have expanded what I wrote at the beginning of 2012 into this present form. The issues surrounding the topic of the sanctity of human life are complex, affect all of us—and stakes are high.

In its earliest form, this book was presented as a paper in the 2012 Apostolic Theological Forum held in Albany, Georgia. It was, admittedly, a hurriedly prepared presentation that I knew would require later revision. With minor edits, it first appeared in the 2012 *Journal of the Apostolic Theological Forum*. Several attendees and presenters felt that the paper should be broadened and published as a stand-alone volume—hopefully with a wide distribution.

It has become apparent to me, and to a number of my ministerial colleagues, that many Christians have no idea how to handle a variety of life and end-of-life situations that eventually present themselves to every family.

These are situations such as:

"The doctors say that there is no hope—should we 'pull the plug' on Dad?"

"The amniocentesis ordered by the doctor shows that our baby will have Down syndrome, and they are pushing us to abort our baby since it will have no quality of life. Isn't abortion wrong?"

"We've tried having a baby, but we were told that it would be impossible unless we try in vitro fertilization. Pastor, what do you think?" (You will see how this question fits the topic later in this book).

"Mom's heart and respiration seem normal, but the doctors told us that she'll never come out of this. They want us to remove her feeding tube. Pastor, what should we do?"

Many saints of God and many pastors are in somewhat of a quandary concerning what to do in a variety of circumstances such as these. Some simply do what others have done, or what their pastor recommended sometime in the past, or what some well-meaning friend or relative recommends; others simply follow the advice of the doctor. But what biblical principles should dictate our actions? Are there serious moral implications in the wake of our decisions?

Of course, earnest prayer should be our first approach—and there certainly are times that God heals what the doctors cannot cure. We have myriad such examples in Apostolic Pentecost. Other times, for whatever reason, God does not heal or intervene miraculously—and we are faced with a decision.

Often, wrong choices or decisions are made that are later either questioned or regretted. Much of the questioning and regret is due to the fact that many saints and pastors are uninformed regarding some of the ethical questions that have arisen with the advent of advances in modern medicine and what biblical principles should be applied. While considerations of medical ethics are taught in schools offering degrees in various medical fields, some of these institutions have instruction or curricula that do not reflect a biblical view of the sanctity of human life.

Generally speaking, evangelical Christians of nearly every stripe—and certainly Apostolic Pentecostals—have been clear about the issue of abortion (with some notable exceptions, including a pastor who was recently elected to public office on a "pro-choice" platform). Abortion, however, is *not* the only issue regarding the sanctity of human life.

The articles of faith of one Apostolic organization include this statement under a subtitle of "Conscientious Scruples": "Mankind is God's earthly image bearer...As reflectors of this divine image, human life has been invested with the highest level of intrinsic value."[1] This is certainly true; and although the statement is contextually applied more to the bearing of arms, the truth of the statement can and should be applied to the broader context of issues wherein human life could be forfeited through action or inaction in a medical setting.

This book is written with the purpose of informing ministry and laity alike of some of the complex issues that face and will face every family in every one of our congregations. This book also seeks to alert believers who work in the medical community to the humanistic influences behind some of the changes being implemented in medical institutions across America. As a pastor, I believe that we pastors have a duty to be informed and aware of what is happening in the world around us. We must become aware of a worldview that is prevalent and growing in modern medicine, academia, government and public media that is quite contrary to Scripture. This prevalent worldview, by reason of its pervasiveness in many parts of our society, will invariably affect our thinking *unless* it is countered with sound, biblical teaching

---

[1] Manual of the United Pentecostal Church International, 2016, (Hazelwood, MO), p. 36

that inculcates a *biblical* worldview as it relates to these issues. Some areas of the United States generally have a more Judeo-Christian mindset than other areas of the country, and the secular worldview described in this book is not as prevalent in those areas. As a result, the medical professions there have not been as deeply affected. Much of the country, however, is profoundly influenced by a culture that devalues human life, and this has infiltrated the healthcare industry.

It is my hope that pastors will read these pages with interest and use this book as a stepping stone to become vitally informed about the issues that face every family. This is so they can wisely counsel families and individuals in their congregations—and teach them these principles *before* their times of need!

Every Christian needs to understand these principles and how they apply to life and end-of-life situations so they will not have to try to digest it all during a time of crisis. With this in mind, I hope that saints of God will take the time to read what is written and become acquainted with the concepts, terms and principles that will help guide them through the labyrinth of complex issues they will someday face. I believe that this will also benefit healthcare workers and medical students within our churches by providing a sound biblical perspective to balance the increasingly secular perspective that some medical schools and journals advance.

I encourage the reader to take the time to read the detailed footnotes as they read through the book. Many of the footnotes will bring clarity or depth to a point being made in the text, and most readers will benefit from taking the time to read them as they work through the book.

I know several saints and ministers who are actively involved in the medical fields—and some of them have seen first-hand the types of scenarios and medical journal articles mentioned in this book and have expressed gratitude for the biblical perspective offered here. Others are fortunate enough to be in areas where doctors and nursing staff routinely offer to pray for their patients before surgeries and other procedures, and have not seen widespread secular influences within the medical professions in their areas. Of course, even in secular hotbeds, there remain many good people in the medical fields who understand the issues and stand against the tide—I am thankful for them.

Nonetheless, the secularist tide is rising, and pressure is being placed upon Christians in the medical community and upon patients in more and more places to acquiesce long-held moral values regarding the inherent sanctity of human life. It is my hope that everyone who reads these pages will find both guidance and an increased understanding of the issues at hand to help you make the right choices.

PFC

Chapter One

The Unthinkable is Happening!

(An Introduction to the Topic)

CR

"But, it will be said that this grand result, in Practical Morals, is a consummation of blessedness that can never be attained without Religion; and that no community will ever be religious, without a Religious Education. Both these propositions, I regard as eternal and immutable truths. Devoid of religious principles and religious affections, the race can never fall so low but that it may sink still lower; animated and sanctified by them, it can never rise so high but that it may ascend still higher."

Horace Mann, 1848

T he very fact that something is *true* often does not hold quite enough sway for most people to believe it. This is especially the case when that which is *true* is also *unthinkable*. With this book, I will attempt to direct a much-needed spotlight on a disturbing truth that has been unthinkable to Apostolics and to our society at large—but is in the process of becoming less disturbing with the desensitization that occurs with the passing of time.

One Nazi official, Hinrich Lohse, said in June of 1943,

"Just imagine that these events were to become known to the enemy! And were being exploited by them! In all probability, such propaganda would be ineffective simply because those hearing and reading it would not be prepared to believe it."[2]

He was speaking, of course, of some of the atrocities of the holocaust—atrocities that, however well documented, are still accounted by some as having never happened.[3]

---

[2] As referenced in Francis A. Schaeffer and Dr. C. Everett Koop, Whatever Happened to the Human Race?, Revised Edition, (Wheaton, IL: Crossway Books, 1983) p.xii

[3] The Committee for Open Debate on the Holocaust (CODOH) and other revisionist groups are very active in denial of a holocaust in

I am not writing, however, about atrocities from which we are removed by decades of time. Rather, I am writing of the present erosion in our own society of the very old biblical and Judeo-Christian ethical standard regarding the sanctity of human life and the atrocities that are the natural consequence of such erosion. It is important that we be aware of this erosion and its resultant abhorrences—for awareness of such an issue is the first step in combatting the insidious forces that eat away at the foundations. And, the sanctity—the sacredness—the value of human life is and must remain foundational in our Apostolic worldview and our broader Judeo-Christian worldview.

We presently live in a world where, in more places than we may realize, it is deemed perfectly acceptable to kill other human beings simply because they have been deemed inconvenient to others; or, because someone determined that their life no longer had any intrinsic value; or, because they represented a burden to others.

While I am speaking of unborn babies and the atrocity of abortion-on-demand, I am also speaking of those who

---

WWII. International meetings (attended by government representatives from several nations), papers, blogs and more are dedicated to such denial of established historical fact regarding the Holocaust.

would euthanize grandma or are doing so because she is a burden (yes, it is happening in Western civilization); or giving a lethal dose of morphine to someone "who is going to die anyway"; or, refusing life-saving treatment for a man because he is over a certain age (or to a child because they have some mental deficiency); or, allowing a Down syndrome newborn to die on a table so that her parents will not have to face the financial and emotional burden of raising her.

These are not the plot lines of a recent sci-fi novel, nor are they the infrequent state of affairs in a few far-flung hospitals in Sweden, or one of the 130 or so memorialized scenes from the life of Dr. Jack Kevorkian. Rather, they represent the growing number of occurrences and "medical" and social decisions that take place *daily* here in North America, in Europe, and across much of our ever-shrinking world.

The crux of the matter is this: There is a great deal of difference between *allowing* someone who is "at death's door" to die and *doing something* to end their life—and this is a line that has become increasingly and purposefully blurred in our society.

In this book I shall present a brief overview of the importance of the biblical understanding of the sanctity of human life: how and why human life is both special and precious; how and why this understanding and ethic is under attack in our current culture; and, why we must be aware of the attack and work to prevent its deepening assault. In particular I will deal with:

1. The biblical view of the sanctity and value of human life, including why life is precious and why "society" has neither the mandate nor the right to dictate when a person's life has supposedly become "devoid of value";[4]

2. The history of the humanistic philosophies[5] that have served to erode the perceived value of human life in the Western culture;

---

[4] The idea that society has both a right and duty to determine when a human life has become "devoid of value" was first set forth in a book published in 1920 by Karl Binding and Alfred Hoche entitled *The Release of the Destruction of Life Devoid of Value: Its Measure and Its Form*. The book was reprinted in English in 1975 by Robert Sassone.

This book was seminal in the formation of a worldview that served to devalue human life—and has been theorized by more than a few to have contributed significantly to the rise of Nazism in the 1930's and 40's. More about this association will appear in the body of this book.

[5] By "humanistic philosophies," I refer to "secular humanism" and even certain aspects of "religious humanism" that tend to dethrone God and deify man as the final arbiter of what is *true* and what is *not*—what is

3. The forces at work in our modern and post-modern culture and institutions that are undermining the perceived value of human life, including the issues of abortion, infanticide, physician-assisted suicide, euthanasia and the philosophical constructs that are making these once-unthinkable acts, both thinkable and doable in our society.

4. Why we, as Apostolic ministers and saints, should sound the warning about the assault upon our societal values regarding human life and the ramifications of the assault upon the lives of those we lead, serve, and/or love.

5. How advances in medical technology have seemingly blurred a line that once seemed clear, and how to apply biblical principles in life choices *and* end-of-life choices—biblical principles that demonstrate the intrinsic value of all human life in the face of such medical advances; and

---

moral and what is *not*. Many prominent humanists, the names of whom are well known in western society over the last 100 years, have codified their belief system, and their means of achieving the advancement of their ideas, in the publishing of the Humanist Manifestos I, III and III, in years 1933, 1973 and 2003 respectively. A more detailed discussion of this follows later in the book.

6. Principles that we should teach people under our care so they will understand the biblical values regarding the sanctity of human life—thus preparing them to make informed decisions regarding important life matters and, especially, end-of-life issues.

a. Why such teaching is critical in a world where there is a growing sentiment that our biblical worldview, including our view of human origin and the value of human life, is ill-informed and unenlightened.

b. Why and how much of the Western healthcare community is learning and imparting bioethical viewpoints to their patients—our congregants—that are quite different from biblical principles, and why God's people must be aware of the changing bioethical standards being touted today among healthcare professionals.

While some regions of the United States still hold to biblical beliefs rather strongly—and this is reflected in the medical community in those areas, many parts of our country have grown increasingly secular and this too is reflected in the medical community. With the increasing mobility of our workforce across the globe, such secular mindsets are influencing an increasingly broad spectrum of our medical institutions. It is a trend that is growing, not diminishing.

Before I get into the biblical constructs of why human life is both special and precious—and why it should be treated with the tenderest of care—I would like to further make the case for the immediate and pressing need of addressing such a topic in a theological setting such as that in which this book was first presented in 2012.

Theology, being the study of God and His Word, finds its value in practical application by people.

In our present society, the technological advances made in medicine are astounding. We now have the means of keeping people alive longer than ever before in the recorded history of the practice of medicine.

Struggles in recent decades over the handling of the well-publicized cases of Karen Ann Quinlan[6] and Terry

---

[6] Karen Ann Quinlan, at age 21, slipped into a coma following a mix of drugs and alcohol, and entered into what doctors called a "persistent vegetative state" (PVS). Doctors told the family that her condition was

Schiavo[7], to name just two, have brought these advances to the forefront in the public mind. The direction taken toward nationalized healthcare under former President Barack Obama and directives issued pursuant to "ObamaCare"[8] were not the final barrage of such measures, regardless of what percentage of those measures are or were rescinded. There is a great deal of pressure to move toward a healthcare system that will ensure so-called "rights" to

irreversible and that she would remain in a PVS for the rest of her life. Following nearly a year, her parents asked that she be removed from the breathing machine she was on and allow her to die. The hospital refused. This started a battle which became highlighted nationally in what became known as the "right to die" cause. In March or 1976 Karen Ann's parents were given the right, by the New Jersey Supreme Court, to "determine her medical treatment, including the right to discontinue all extraordinary means of life support." She was removed from the ventilator over a period of five days—yet remained alive for another nine years—dying of pneumonia in 1985. The creation of the "living wills" (also called an "advance directive") is attributed to the case. See www.karenannquinlanhospice.org/history.

[7] The Terry Schiavo case is another case involving someone who slipped in to a PVS. Following eight years, her husband sought permission to have her feeding tube removed and to allow her to die. Her parents challenged and a long series of court battles ensued—ending with her feeding tube being removed on March 18, 2005 and her dying on March 31, 2005. The Schiavo case brought the "right-to-die" cause back into the national spotlight, and involved such nationally-recognized personalities into the fray as 2012 Presidential candidate and Operation Rescue founder, Randall Terry and, then, President George W. Bush. See www.terrisfight.org

[8] ObamaCare is officially known as *The Patient Protection and Affordable Care Act* which was signed into Federal law on March 23, 2010 by U.S. President, Barack Hussein Obama II. See http://www.conservapedia.com/ObamaCare

abortion, infanticide and euthanasia in America and throughout western civilization. I will substantiate that statement later in this book. Incidentally, it seems that this pressure toward socialized medicine is viewed negatively by most of the dedicated health professionals whom I have met. Yet this is not stopping the political left from pushing this agenda onto a largely resistant healthcare industry. Of course, there are those within the healthcare community who are pushing the same agenda from within.

In recent years, the debate regarding the trend toward socialized medicine and its postured ill-regard for the sanctity of human life was brought to the national stage when a caller to the conservative Mark Levin radio talk show identified himself as a Chicago-based neurosurgeon who had recently returned from a meeting of neurological surgeons in Washington, D.C. wherein his group was purportedly briefed on *"Obama's 'Healthcare Plan for Advanced Neurological Care'"* issued by the U. S. Department of Health and Human Services (HHS).

The caller, who identified himself as "Jeff," stated that they were told, and that a non-publicly-available document published by HHS stated, "basically...that if you're over 70 and you come into an emergency room (for something requiring stroke or aneurism therapy), and you are on government-supported care—that you're going to get 'comfort care.'" He went on to state that the document uses the term "units" instead of the more personal term, "patients;" and that the document states clearly that "for patients [units] over 70 years of age—advanced neurosurgical care was not generally indicated."[9]

The call, on November 22, 2011, prompted a great deal of media chatter in the days and weeks following, with people claiming that the man was a hoax, and with others contending there were clear indications that the man, who was vetted by the show staff—and appropriately so—was indeed the real deal.[10]

---

[9] An audio file of the show was downloaded at http://marklevinshow.com/Article.asp?id=2339236&spid=41445, with the referenced portion occurring between the runtime of 44:35 and 49:16. A transcript was found at http://marklevinfan.com/2011/11/24/ obamacare-death-panels-are-coming/. The call, according to Levin at runtime 51:00-51:05, was "vetted" by his staff and they verified that the caller "is who he says he is." Audio and transcript retrieved November 27, 2015 and January 2, 2012, respectively.

[10] Related media articles and blog posts were numerous—and were clearly divided along ideological lines. Intrinsic information in the transcript indicates that the man possessed knowledge that further identifies him as a legitimate caller. FactCheck.org, as of November 27, 2016, has updated statements indicating that the caller was not who he said he was, and that the reported document does not actually exist. Regardless of whether the call was legitimate in the information it purported, it is clear that the call touched off a lot of interest in both

Whether the call and its content were legitimate, the reaction to it certainly called attention to societal fears that were (and still are) simmering under the surface. While some may look at such a call as "conspiracy theories run amok," there has been a great deal of talk at some very high levels regarding the likes of a mandatory *duty to die* for those who have a life that is deemed *devoid of value*.[11] It has been going on for a number of years.

Consider that none other than the famous co-discoverer of DNA, proud signer of the Humanist Manifesto II, and Nobel prize recipient, Francis Crick, called in 1978 "for a new ethical system, featuring abortion and infanticide, which would [also] make it mandatory for all persons over eighty years of age to be put to death."[12] One wonders if Crick changed his mind as he passed into his 80's—Crick died at the age of eighty-eight. Consider also the following quote:

"right-to-life/pro-life" groups and those with a more progressive agenda.

[11] More on the terms "duty to die" and "life devoid of value" will follow later in the book.

[12] Herbert Schlossberg, Idols for Destruction: The Conflict of Christian Faith and American Culture (Wheaton, IL: Crossway Books, 1990), p.80

"Margaret Sanger, who was the original founder of Planned Parenthood, famously said, 'The most merciful thing a large family can do for one of its infant members is kill it.' Nobel Prize Laureate James Watson, co-discoverer of DNA [along with Crick]—hardly fringe—said, 'Because of the limitations of present detection methods, most birth defects are not discovered until birth; however, if a child was not declared alive until three days after birth, the doctor could allow the child to die, if the parents so chose, and save a lot of misery and suffering.'"[13]

Note the absolute dismissal of any idea that a child with a birth defect could have a life with any intrinsic value.

One college textbook, written by a humanist and one-time professor of philosophy at what is now Oklahoma State University, stated that "no child should be admitted into the society of the living who would be certain to suffer any social handicap—for example," he said, "any physical

---

[13] http://hankhanegraaff.blogspot.com/, February 21, 2011 post entry.

or mental defect that would prevent marriage or would make others tolerate his company only from a sense of mercy."[14] This was written over a half-century ago, and is still cited in literature of our day.

Thomas Sowell, celebrated conservative author and "scholar in residence" at the Hoover Institution, Stanford University, recently wrote the following at the beginning of his editorial piece in *National Review Online*, titled with the question, *"A Duty to Die?:"*

"One of the many fashionable notions that have caught on among some of the intelligentsia is that old people have "a duty to die" rather than become a burden to others.

This is more than just an idea discussed around a seminar table. Already the government-run medical system in Britain is restricting what medications or treatments it will authorize for the elderly. Moreover, it seems almost certain that similar attempts to contain runaway costs will lead to similar

---

[14] Millard Spencer Everette, Ideals for Life (New York, NY: Wiley, 1954) p.346ff, as cited in Schlossberg, p.80

policies when American medical care is taken over by the government."[15]

Truly, this seems to substantiate the allegations that our society and government—by virtue of their humanistic leanings and ideals—are indeed slouching toward an ethic that devalues human life if that life is deemed "inconvenient" to those around them. Thomas Sowell cannot be passed off as a right-wing conspiracy-theory lunatic: He is the author of many scholarly books; has taught at such prestigious academic institutions as Cornell, Harvard, Amherst and Stanford; and has written frequently for the Wall Street Journal, Forbes and Fortune magazines. He also writes a syndicated column that appears in newspapers across the United States.

These are *frightening* thoughts—*unthinkable* ponderings—yet they are the realities that are encroaching into the lives of those to whom we minister and who attend our churches. We had best be aware of the onslaught of this pervasive slide of moral sensibilities and prepare ourselves and our people to make the right choices at difficult times.

---

[15] http://www.nationalreview.com/articles/229733/duty-die/thomas-sowell, May 11, 2010

Bioethical questions that are brought to the forefront in the midst of the humanistic ideals of our society's culture affect more than end-of-life issues—they also affect issues such as how to deal with infertility during the early years of trying to have a family. These are questions that will, in one manner or another, affect every family within our congregations.

Some of the challenges we face are the result of medical advances and the seeming ability to keep people alive unnaturally and mechanically when no curative treatment is medically possible. These challenges have caused at least one theologian-author to intone: "Many bioethical decisions simply do not have one absolutely binding right or wrong answer."[16] He may be right; however, there *are* biblical principles that, if applied to our lives, will help us navigate the crucial life-decisions from a biblical perspective and may well keep us in right standing with our Lord.

---

[16] David VanDrunen, Bioethics and the Christian Life: A Guide to Making Difficult Decisions (Wheaton, IL: Crossway Books, 2009), p.16

Chapter Two

The Biblical View of the Sanctity of Human Life

"Thus saith the LORD, thy redeemer, and he that formed thee from the womb, I *am* the LORD that maketh all *things;* that stretcheth forth the heavens alone; that spreadeth abroad the earth by myself."

Isaiah 44:24

The Scriptures give us our understanding of and respect for the sanctity of human life. When I speak of its "sanctity," I am speaking of the fact that human life has intrinsic value because we were created in the image of God and because *He* has placed such value on human life.

In Genesis 2 the Scriptures expand upon the creation of mankind, mentioned briefly in the first chapter of our Bible. Both chapters give us important information regarding the nature of what God did in the creation of man—and the *value* He placed upon that most-special of His creations:

> And God said, Let us make man *in our image, after our likeness*: and let them have dominion over the fish of the sea, and over the fowl of the air, and over the cattle, and over all the earth, and over every creeping thing that creepeth upon the earth. So God created man *in his own image, in the image of God created he him*; male and female created he them. And God blessed them, and God said unto them, Be fruitful, and multiply, and replenish the earth, and subdue

it: and have dominion over the fish of the sea, and over the fowl of the air, and over every living thing that moveth upon the earth (Genesis 1:26-28).

And the LORD God formed man of the dust of the ground, and breathed into his nostrils the breath of life; *and man became a living soul* (Genesis 2:7).

These two passages at the beginning of our Bibles are referenced, directly or indirectly, several times throughout the Holy Writ. Man was not created as the other life that surrounds us on the earth. There are three things in particular that distinguish us decidedly from all other life— be it animal, plant, or the microscopic life that seems to fit neither taxonomical niche:

1. Man was made in the image and likeness of God, after His similitude;

2. Man was made a "living soul." That is, every human possesses an integral *soul* that was destined to abide forever following his or her creation; and

3. Man was given dominion over the rest of creation, in particular over all other life upon the

earth. We are, in this respect quite unlike the life of plants or animals.

We are distinct in these ways—and these are *significant* differences. For the sake of brevity, I shall only address one of these points below:

Made in the Image of God

The fact that man is made in the image of God is not a minor issue. Much has been written about this, and it is not necessary that I deal with this in detail as it is a readily understood point among Apostolics. There are a few thoughts, however, that I would like to point out for our discussion. First, it was not merely Adam and Eve who were made in the image of God—but all of mankind. What is so clearly stated in Genesis 1:27 and Genesis 5:1 is reiterated when James reminds us that all men are "made after the similitude of God."[17] While mankind lost some of their glory in the fall of man[18], we still maintain a certain "image and glory of God (I Corinthians 11:7)."[19] It is not

---

[17] James 3:9 KJV

[18] Romans 6:23 – "For all have sinned, and come short of the glory of God;" (KJV)

[19] Barnes' Notes on the Bible states concerning this phrase in I Corinthians 11:7 (emphasis mine), "The phrase 'the image of God'

that we are pure as *He* is pure, but rather that we generally maintain other aspects that resemble our Creator, such as the ability to reason and make judgments; to feel and demonstrate a range of emotions such as love, hate, jealousy; and more. We also resemble the only bodily form that the Creator took upon Himself: "the form of a servant...made in the likeness of men" (Philippians 2:7).[20]

Beyond this there is one aspect that is rarely approached theologically, but given the issue at hand, this aspect seems especially important to consider: As one author put it, man was made "to *live eschatologically!*"[21] He went on to say that "human beings are *destined for life.*"[22] By this it is meant that the Scriptures make it clear

---

refers to the fact that man was made in the likeness of his Maker Gen. 1:27; and proves that, though fallen, *there is a sense in which he is still the image of God.* It is not because man is truly [righteous] or pure, and thus resembles his Creator; but it evidently is because he was invested by his Maker with authority and dominion; he was superior to all other creatures; Gen. 1:28."

[20] Adam was the "figure," the "die as struck," the "image" of "him that was to come;" that is of Christ Jesus (Romans 5:14). It seems that this verse is actually stating that Adam was formed physically after the pattern of Jesus Christ; the Creator looking *proleptically* into the future when the Christ would be born—and patterning Adam after that "image."

[21] The term "eschatologically" is used here to simply mean that which applies to *eternity*—and not to "end time" events as the term is often used.

[22] VanDrunen, p.46

that mankind was originally created to live forever. Consider the narrative near the end of Genesis 3:

> And the LORD God said, Behold, the man is become as one of us, to know good and evil: and now, lest he put forth his hand, and take also of the tree of life, and eat, and live for ever: Therefore the LORD God sent him forth from the garden of Eden, to till the ground from whence he was taken. So *he drove out the man*; and he placed at the east of the garden of Eden Cherubims, and a flaming sword which turned every way, *to keep the way of the tree of life* (Genesis 3:22-24).

Man, from the beginning, was created to live forever. He was created, as VanDrunen said, to "live an *eschatological* life!" [23] This is not true of the animals among God's creation. Death came as a result of the curse—and it came as an enemy, not a friend. This enemy called death loses its sting *only* through the gospel[24]—yet this is only because the physical death of our bodies

---

[23] Ibid., p.48
[24] I Corinthians 15:50-57

35

becomes the passageway to eternal life in Jesus Christ! Without the gospel, death is a dreaded thing. It is an unnatural thing in that man was created to live forever—and when a man dies who is not born of the water and of the Spirit—their physical death becomes a passage way to an eternal death—an eschatological death! Death is an unnatural imposition upon humankind—something that was not part of the original design for man.

I belabor this point a bit so we can understand that the language of the humanistic framework used in our society—and in the medical community in particular—is not in line with the Word of God. Literature of our day regarding preparation for dying and hospice care speaks frequently, and without regard to the gospel, that "death is a natural part of life," that "death is natural—and not something to fear."

As Scott Stiegemeyer stated in his March 21, 2008 blog post for Concordia Theological Seminary,

> Death is unnatural in the sense that it is not the <u>design</u> of the Creator. It's not supposed to happen to you. When God created Adam and Eve in the Garden, it was not His purpose for them to die. Death is not

just a part of the "circle of life" as in that horrible Disney song. Holy Scripture describes death as the curse for sin (Romans 5).

As a thing unnatural, death is not something I am willing to make peace with. There will be no coming to terms. No armistice. Contrary to the well-intentioned but ethically challenged right-to-die crowd, death is not a friend to be welcomed as the deliverer from this world's troubles.[25]

Paul reminds us in I Corinthians 15:26 that "the last enemy that shall be destroyed is death." Death is our enemy—not a friend in the circle of life. Only for those who have prepared themselves through obedience to the gospel does Paul's proclamation—"for me to live is Christ, and to die is gain"—become a reality. Yet nowhere does even the Christian have the license to hasten its coming.

---

[25]   http://seminaryblog.com/2008/03/is-death-a-natural-part-of-life/, Accessed December 17, 2012.

From the Moment of Conception

As will be noted in Chapter 4, western society's prevailing Judeo-Christian perspective has long held that human life is precious from the moment of conception. In fact, doctors who have taken, upon their graduation from medical school, a form of the Hippocratic Oath (as adopted in the Declaration of Geneva – 1948) have included a phrase to that effect for many years. This point of view appears clear in the Scriptures.

The LORD said that He knew Jeremiah before he was even formed, and that he was called to be a prophet even while in his mother's womb (Jeremiah 1:5). Consider also the Holy-Ghost-inspired words of the "Sweet Psalmist of Israel," David (emphasis mine):

"For thou hast possessed my reins: thou hast covered me *in my mother's womb*. I will praise thee; for I am fearfully and wonderfully made: marvellous are thy works; and that my soul knoweth right well. My substance was not hid from thee, when I was made in secret, and curiously wrought in the lowest parts of the earth. Thine eyes did see my substance, yet being unperfect;

and *in thy book all my members were written, which in continuance were fashioned, when as yet there was none of them"* (Psalms 139:13-16).

In this Psalm, David speaks of himself in pronouns reflective of him *as a person.* He said it was *"me"* in *"my"* mother's womb; he said that *"I"* was made in secret, and that all *"my"* members (parts) were written..."when as yet there were none of them." In that initial single-celled embryo (zygote - the combining of two haploid cells into one cell), all of the DNA of David was "written"—just as the Psalmist said. He was "David" from the moment of conception—and God knew him! So it is with every human being.

There has been some challenge on a scientific basis to this premise and some supposition that the traditional understanding of the foregoing passages is in error. I would like to briefly address these issues here.

First, as mentioned above, the moment that an ovum is fertilized it produces a single-celled zygote that contains the unique DNA structure of the person who will be later recognized by those who will know them by their traits. Yet, some have postulated: "What if that zygote develops into a multi-celled embryo (blastocyst) that then splits into twins?" These are known as monozygotic or "identical" twins. Generally, monozygotic twins can develop anywhere within the first 14 or so days following conception. The argument, therefore, is that we cannot say that this blastocyst is an individual person, a human being, until "twinning" either does or does not occur. While this may sound like a plausible argument on the surface, we shall see that it does not hold water.

First, as Gilbert Meilaender states in *Bioethics: A Primer for Christians*, "The argument supposes that where once there was simply *X*, a collection of cells, there are now *Tom* and *Tim*. But metaphysically, it is just as possible that where once there was *Tom* there are now *Tom* and *Tim*, and it seems unlikely that science can tell us why this should not be the case."[26] It could also be understood that God alone knows whether a blastocyst will—according to His prerogative—separate into twins or not, and in His book "all his/her/their members were written, which in continuance were fashioned, when as yet there was none of them."

---

[26] Gilbert Meilaender, Bioethics: A Primer for Christians, Third Edition (Grand Rapids, MI: Eerdmans, 2013), p.31

Meilaender went on to make a salient point:

"Moreover, advancing knowledge of embryological development indicates that the beginnings of the mammalian body plan are laid down from the time of fertilization. The newly fertilized ovum sets up an equivalent axis in the embryo. Thus for example, where the feet and head will sprout is established in the first hours after egg and sperm unite. Even the earliest embryo, it seems, is more than just a featureless collection of cells; it is an integrated, self-developing organism, capable (if all goes well) of the continued development that characterizes human life—we are right to react with awe and wonder at the mystery of its individual existence."[27]

I cannot help but to concur! This is, once again, a place where science confirms what was written in the Scriptures long before the discovery of DNA and the ability to begin

---

[27] Ibid.

to look into the intricacies of the development of human life.

An additional point worth noting should be called to our attention. So-called "pro-choice" advocates are fond of proclaiming "a woman's right to choose" and will use misleading phrases such as "every woman has a right to choose what she does with her body." Is this a point of view that should be taken by a biblical Christian? The answer is a clear and decisive "no!" First, we are *not* our own, for we were bought with a price. The Scriptures boldly declare that both our body and our spirit belong to God and not to ourselves. Yet beyond this is the more relevant point to our discussion: An unborn fetus, regardless of how far it has advanced in the gestational process, is NOT part of the mother's body! Every part—every *cell*—of the mother has the same DNA, but every part—every *cell*—of that unborn baby has its *own* DNA. Advocates of abortion-on-demand are fond of declaring an "unwanted fetus" as something no more than unneeded extra "tissue" that can be discarded at will. To say and believe this is to disregard the facts. This is a common belief in our postmodern society, a carefully-inculcated belief—and, in this book, I hope to dispel it as groundless and as contrary to the Scriptures.

A proper biblical understanding of the inherent sanctity of a human life from the moment of conception should be enough to guide a sincere heart through such potential situations of unanticipated pregnancies, cases of incest, rape, and supposed instances of a choice needing to be made to abort a baby in order to save the life of an expectant mother.

The *Dublin Declaration on Maternal Health* of 2012, signed by a large number of practicing obstetricians and gynecologists, makes a bold statement that is quite contrary to the typical soundbites we hear from leftist media outlets: "As experienced practitioners and researchers in obstetrics and gynecology, we affirm that direct abortion – the purposeful destruction of the unborn child – is not medically necessary to save the life of a woman.

"We uphold that there is a fundamental difference between abortion, and necessary medical treatments that are carried out to save the life of the mother, even if such treatment results in the loss of life of her unborn child....We confirm that the prohibition of abortion does not affect, in any way, the availability of optimal care to pregnant women."[28] I applaud these medical professionals for boldly standing up to the leftist trend in much of Western society that devalues the lives of the unborn.

As early as 1967, Dr. Alan Guttmacher,[29] known as the father of Planned Parenthood, candidly acknowledged: "Today it is possible for almost any patient to be brought through pregnancy alive, unless she suffers from a fatal illness such as cancer or leukemia, and, if so, abortion would be unlikely to prolong, much less save, life."[30]

Yet there are indeed rare situations where the life of an expectant mother may necessitate the life of the unborn being taken. If you will take a closer look at part of the *Dublin Declaration* above, it *distinguishes* between an abortion as "the purposeful destruction of the unborn child" and "necessary medical treatments...to save the life of the mother, *even if such treatment results in the loss of life of her unborn child.*" Even Guttmacher's statement draws this

---

[28] http://afterabortion.org/2014/doctors-abortion-not-necessary-to-save-mothers-lives/, Accessed December 15, 2016.
[29] Guttmacher served as president of Planned Parenthood and vice-president of the American Eugenics Society.
[30] Alan F. Guttmacher, "Abortion:Yesterday, Today and Tomorrow," in *The Case for Legalized Abortion Now* (Berkeley: CA.: Diablo Press,1967).

distinction, although many pro-life groups fail to recognize it.

One important example is that of an ectopic pregnancy. An ectopic pregnancy is that in which the embryo becomes implanted somewhere other than in the uterus—most often in the fallopian tubes that connect the ovaries to the uterus. In the case of *abdominal* ectopic pregnancies, these have sometimes been carried to full term, but such cases are very rare, and in some cases they can present a serious risk to the mother's life. In the event of a fallopian ectopic pregnancy, if the embryo does not move within a short timeframe down the tube to the uterus, there is a significant likelihood that the growing fetus could burst the fallopian tube, thus causing internal bleeding that threatens the life of the mother.

I know of one pastor who was approached for counsel regarding this very issue. The couple was given a window of time by medical professionals in a non-emergency situation, and he asked them to allow him to pray over the issue during that window. He prayed that the embryo would travel to the uterus and be fine. When the woman went back to the doctor at the end of that window that is exactly what had happened. Of course such a result cannot be counted upon in every instance—yet as Christians we ought to do our best to follow the admonition of the Scriptures: "Do not be anxious about anything, but in everything by prayer and supplication with thanksgiving let your requests be made known to God" (Philippians 4:6, ESV).

According to AbortionFacts.com (which is operated as a pro-life website), less than one percent of all abortions performed in the United States are done to save the life of the mother.[31]

A common argument in the pro-choice movement is to bring up the rare cases involving an attempt to spare a mother's life. As mentioned on AbortionFacts.com, "Since every abortion kills an innocent human being, it is morally abhorrent to use the rare cases when abortion is necessary to save the life of the mother as justification for the millions of on demand 'convenience' abortions."[32] This type of rhetoric from the pro-choice camp is a common propaganda tool.

The majority of abortions performed in America and beyond are elective. Statistics vary among sources but, generally, the top reasons for women getting abortions

---

[31] http://www.abortionfacts.com/facts/8, Accessed December 17, 2016.
[32] Ibid.

include inadequate finances, not being ready for the responsibility, the anticipation of too dramatic of a change of life, adult relationship issues, the age or maturity of the mother, and the lack of or failure of contraception.[33,34] In the final analysis, virtually all of these reasons are matters of convenience or irresponsibility, and the option of abortion is simply a perceived escape from accountability and personal responsibility.

If someone is unable or unwilling to care for a baby, or if a baby is unwanted due to the trauma of rape, there will certainly be someone who would adopt that baby and give him or her a chance at life. I know of several Apostolic families who have adopted children and raised them in the fear and admonition of the Lord.

Tragic situations can arise—calling for a choice to be made. It would do expectant parents well to have the following advice instilled as a guiding principal when faced with such a predicament:

"When two lives are threatened and only one can be saved, doctors must always save

[33] Ibid.
[34] http://www.johnstonsarchive.net/policy/abortion/abreasons.html, Accessed December 17, 2016.

that life....If the mother has a fast-spreading uterine cancer, the surgery to remove the cancer may result in the loss of the child's life. In an ectopic pregnancy the child is developing outside the uterus...and may have to be removed to save his mother's life....These are tragic situations, but even if one life must be lost, the life that can be saved should be. More often than not, that life is the mother's, not the child's. There are rare cases in later stages of pregnancy when the mother can't be saved, but the baby can....Again, one life saved is better than two lost."[35]

I believe that most doctors would wholeheartedly agree with the above statement. The dominant voices among the pro-choice movement would like for us to believe that this moral ethic is broken and that mothers with ectopic pregnancies are at serious risk because of the stance of the prolife camp. Nothing could be further from the truth.

---

[35] http://www.abortionfacts.com/facts/8, Accessed December 17, 2016.

The fact of the matter is that an innocent child in the womb is a precious human life, and regardless of the circumstances that brought about that life, it is to be protected and valued. If both lives can be saved, then every means of doing so should be employed. If not, the physician is obligated to save the life that can be saved.

Every Christian should understand fully that the inherent sanctity of human life is clearly spelled out in the Word of God and should be valued by each of us, regardless of our present situation.

Chapter Three

How the "Culture of Death" Developed

"The invalid is a parasite on society. In a certain state it is indecent to go on living. To vegetate on in cowardly dependence on physicians and medicaments after the meaning of life, the *right* to life, has been lost ought to entail the profound contempt of society. Physicians...ought to be the communicators of this contempt—not prescriptions, but every day a fresh dose of *disgust* with their patients.... To create a new responsibility, that of the physician, in all cases in which the highest interest of life, of *ascending* life, demands the most ruthless suppression and sequestration of degenerating life—for examples in determining the right to reproduce, the right to be born, the right to live."

Friedrich Nietzsche, 1889

W e shall not go back to the beginning, but we shall look at the development and advancement of philosophies in our Western society that have gained prominence through the last few centuries—and have accelerated in the last 100 years to become the veritable bane of our present society.

Kant and Hegel

In 21st-century America, very few are familiar with the writings of Georg Hegel and Immanuel Kant, yet the philosophies that they set forth in the late 18th and early 19th centuries gave rise to realities that affect every part of our Western society. While Kant was influenced by the likes of Spinoza and others, and while Kant, in turn, influenced Hegel—I will begin our discussion starting with Immanuel Kant—a man of Scottish ancestry and German upbringing. Kant initially began studying under the ministry of a Pietist sect (similar to early Methodism) and was invited to enter the ministry,[36] but he seemed to despise that early instruction and moved toward studies

---

[36] Will and Ariel Durant, The Story of Civilization, Volume X – Rousseau and Revolution (New York, NY: Simon and Schuster, 1967), p.531

regarding logic, science and metaphysics. Most of his early writing (1740 through 1762) was related to science, but he later branched into theology with the treatise, *The Only Possible Ground for Proving the Existence of God.*[37] It was not until 1781 that he published *Critique of Pure Reason*, a work that was twelve years in the making. It was a work that historian and self-described atheist Will Durant, branded as "one of the most destructive analyses that the Christian theology has ever received."[38]

Kant reasoned that "the things of the world must be viewed as if they received their existence from a highest intelligence. The idea [of God] is thus really a heuristic, not an ostensive, concept...."[39] He went on to reason that the more imperative reason for religious belief is that such religious belief is "indispensable to morality." He said, "If there is no primordial being, distinct from the world, if the world is...without an Author, if our will is not free, if the soul is...perishable matter, then the moral ideas and principles lose all validity."

---

[37] Ibid., p.534
[38] Ibid., p.535
[39] Immanuel Kant, Critique of Pure Reason, 1st Edition, p. 671 as cited in Durant, p.538

He was in essence stating that we are justified in creating God so that morality has meaning. He actually stated it this way: "We are justified in representing the cause of the world in terms of an anthropomorphism...namely as a being that has understanding, feelings of pleasure and displeasure, and desires and volitions corresponding to these."[40]

In a later work, published in 1785 and entitled *Fundamental Principles of the Metaphysic of Morals*, he attempts to further couch feelings related to morality in terms of the functions of human reasoning. He asked, "Whence have we the conception of God as the supreme good?" He answers his own question, "Simply from the idea of moral perfection, which reason frames a priori,[41] and connects inseparably with the notion of a free-will."[42]

He later stated in his *Critique of Practical Reason* in 1788 that "it is clear that all moral conceptions have their

---

[40] Ibid., p.468; 700 as cited in Durant, p.539

[41] "a priori" means that which is "existing in the mind prior to and independent of experience;" "not based on study or prior examination." Dictionary.com. Dictionary.com Unabridged. Random House, Inc. http://dictionary.reference.com/browse/a priori (accessed: January 10, 2012).

[42] Immanuel Kant; Ed. by C.A. Sainte-Beauve, Fundamental Principles of the Metaphysics of Morals; The Harvard Classics (New York, NY: P.F. Collier & Son, 1910) p.320

seat and origin completely a priori in the reason."[43] His concept of God was *not* that God created man—but that man created God. One of his writings, published after his death, made this abundantly clear:

> God is not a substance existing outside me, but merely a moral relation within me...The categorical imperative does not assume a substance issuing its commands from on high, conceived therefore as outside me, but is a commandment or prohibition of my own reason.[44]

Thus the fundamental idea of Kant's "critical philosophy" was "human autonomy"—the idea that man's morality and ultimate destiny are derived from his own ability to reason. This is the basis for the widespread humanistic thought that pervades our modern institutions; be they institutions of government, education, public media, healthcare or more. Immanuel Kant has been called *"the central figure* in modern philosophy."[45] Men like Fitche, Hegel and Schelling "built [their] metaphysical

---

[43] Durant, p.541
[44] Ibid., p550
[45] http://plato.stanford.edu/entries/kant/

castles upon the…idealism of Kant."[46] Indeed, Germany's literature (and later, literature throughout much of Europe, and later still, the United States) soon began to feel Kant's influence,[47] for—as historian Will Durant noted—"the philosophy of one age is likely to be the literature of the next."[48]

Georg Wilhelm Friedrich Hegel followed on the heels of Kant in saying: "Pure reason, incapable of any limitation, is the Deity itself."[49] One of the formulations for which he is best noted is the "dialectic" (literally, the art of conversation) of "thesis, antithesis and synthesis." This is essentially the idea that "an idea or situation potentially contains its opposite, develops it, struggles against it, then unites with it to take another transient form."[50] This is the philosophical construct that is the genesis for modern "situational ethics" being taught in schools throughout our country today. The way Hegel's theory works is that an idea is put forth (that which appears to be a *truth*); this is

---

[46] Durant, p.551
[47] Will and Ariel Durant, The Story of Civilization, Volume XI – The Age of Napoleon (New York, NY: Simon and Schuster, 1975), p.658
[48] Ibid.
[49] Walter Kauffmann, Hegel: Reinterpretation, Texts and Commentary, New York, NY: Doubleday, 1965), p.61
[50] Durant, Volume XI, p.649

called the *thesis*. Then a "truth" that is the *opposite* of that apparent truth (the *antithesis*) is voiced and struggles against the thesis until it is blended with it, forming a *synthesis* (a NEW *truth*). This new "truth" is now the new "thesis" against which an antithesis is formed—and the cycle goes on. In Hegel's construct there is no "truth" that is inviolable. In this way of thinking, there are no "absolute" truths: all truth is *situational* and subject to question. One wonders if Hegel believed his idea was inviolably "true."

From Kant to Humanism

Kant and Hegel and their brand of philosophy gave rise to the exploits of natural scientist Alexander von Humboldt (arguably the most "famous" person in the world during the general age that produced the likes of George Washington, Benjamin Franklin, Thomas Jefferson and Napoleon Bonaparte).[51,52] Von Humboldt was the chief inspiration

[51] David McCullough, Brave Companions (New York, NY: Simon & Schuster, 1992), p.5
[52] Gerald Helferich, Humboldt's Cosmos (New York, NY: Gotham, 2004), p.xvii; the timeframe of von Humboldt's popularity overlapped that of Jefferson and Bonaparte, began about the time of Washington's death (2 years after Washington's Presidency ended), and about 8 years following Franklin's death. von Humboldt has at least 12 species, 10

for Charles Darwin and his studies that lead to *"On the Origin of the Species."*[53] It was said that Darwin carried three books with him during his travels on the Beagle to inspire him: "...the Bible, Milton and Humboldt."[54] He said that he "almost adore[d]" Humboldt.[55] Kant and Hegel also created the framework for Karl Marx, his *Communist Manifesto*, and the advent of Marxist socialism as well as for German philosopher Friedrich Nietzsche and his ideas of the "Superman" which would survive only by "human selection, by eugenic foresight and an ennobling education."[56] Kantian/Hegelian philosophy gave birth to Marxism and to Darwinian and neo-Darwinian evolution— and together these gave birth to Nietzsche's philosophies and the thought that *man*, and not God, is the final arbiter of Truth and the master of human destiny. This worldview is the *foundation* of the godless, liberal, humanistic mindset

geographical features, 21 places, 16 universities, colleges or schools, a sea on the Moon, and an asteroid named for him. Places that bear his name appear in Europe, North, Central and South America, on the Moon and in the heavens. His influence remains widely felt, though his name means little to most Americans today.
[53] McCullough, p.5
[54] Ibid.
[55] Helferich, p.xviii
[56] Will Durant, The Story of Philosophy (New York, NY: Simon & Schuster, 1961), p.319

that dominates the educational and governmental elite in Western societies. It is a worldview that has been codified, amplified and put into action. It is affecting our society in countless ways, and therefore—whether we realize it or not—is affecting *us*.

Humanistic Influence in Western (Including American) Society

John Dewey (1859-1952), the "father of American progressive education" and, in essence, the father of the American public school system as we know it, was a champion of secular humanism (he is believed to have written most of the Humanist Manifesto (Humanist Manifesto I)). He was an ardent Darwinian evolutionist who wrote about the supposed relationship between Darwinian evolution and ethics, the relationship of education to ethics, and the advancement of his ideas of "social progress and reform."[57,58] Dewey looked at the development of a public school system as the primary means of promoting his humanistic ideals. In his famed

---

[57] John Dewey, Early Works of John Dewey (Carbondale, IL: SIUP, 1972), pp.34, 54
[58] http://dewey.pragmatism.org/creed.htm, Accessed December 18, 2016.

"Pedagogical Creed," Article Five: The School and Social Progress, he was clear about his vision of changing society through education. He wrote (emphasis mine):

> "I believe that education is the fundamental method of social progress and reform...I believe that all reforms which rest simply on the enactment of law, or the threatening of certain penalties, or upon changes in mechanical or outward arrangements, are transitory and futile...that the adjustment of individual activity on the basis of social consciousness [which he suggests be developed, en masse, in individuals through the public education system] is the only sure method of social reconstruction."[59]

Note the terms "social progress and reform," and "social reconstruction." Dewey believed strongly in the elimination from our society of the idea of a supreme being with inviolable standards. He said, "There is nothing left worth preserving in the notions of unseen powers,

---

[59] Ibid.

controlling human destiny, to which obedience and worship are due."[60]

His philosophy for "social reconstruction"—the reshaping of our society—was much the same as that of Adolf Hitler, who said, "He alone, who owns the youth, gains the future."[61] "When an opponent declares, 'I will not come over to your side,' I say calmly, 'Your child belongs to us already. What are you? You will pass on. Your descendants, however, now stand in the new camp. In a short time they will know nothing but this new community'."[62]

Note the humanistic bent of his doctrine, "I begin with the young. We older ones are used up...but my magnificent youngsters! Are there any finer ones in the world? Look at these young men and boys! What material! With them, I can make a New World. This is the heroic stage of youth. Out of it will come the creative man, the man-god."[63] Some may see it as a stretch to tie the thinking of Immanuel Kant,

[60] John Dewey, Larry A. Hickman, Thomas M. Alexander, The Essential Dewey, Volume 1, Pragmatism, Education Democracy (Bloomington, IN: Indiana University Press, 1998), p.403
[61] Adolf Hitler. BrainyQuote.com, Xplore Inc, 2012. http://www.brainyquote.com/quotes/quotes/a/adolfhitle378177.html
[62] From a speech made November 6, 1933.
[63] http://www.oppapers.com/essays/The-Hitler-Youth/329966

Friedrich Nietzsche, John Dewey and Adolf Hitler together—but the fact remains that the thinking of the latter two was derived largely from the former two and others who followed them. I am certainly not the only one who believes that the underpinnings of our Western society's humanistic bent on the violability of human life stems from Kant, Nietzsche, Dewey and Hitler. Following my original analysis of this in my 2012 paper, author David Gushee wrote along similar lines (in more detail than here) in Chapters 7 and 8 of his fascinating book, *The Sacredness of Human Life: Why an Ancient Biblical Vision is Key to the World's Future.*

The Unthinkable Becomes Thinkable

What was *unthinkable* to Americans and much of the Western world in Hitler's day was the *natural progression* of the indoctrination of Hitler's Kantian/Hegelian philosophy when all other doctrines were removed from their thoughts. Through the medium of the Hitler Youth, whose numbers swelled from 1,200 to nearly 7.3 million during the pre-war era of 1923 to 1939,[64] Adolf Hitler was

---

[64] http://www.historyplace.com/worldwar2/hitleryouth/hj-timeline.htm

able to indoctrinate an entire generation of German youth and take them from a worldview in which mass genocide was *unthinkable* to one that allowed them to carry out mass genocide for what they believed, largely, to be a righteous cause. In *a single generation*, a blatant disregard for the sanctity of human life was spawned and utilized with consummate efficiency once their moral foundations had been removed through education and replaced with a new idea. It was, perhaps, in Hitler's thinking, the "antithesis" to the biblically moral "thesis."

As suggested by Christian philosopher Francis A. Schaeffer and former U.S. Surgeon General C. Everett Koop in their epoch book, *Whatever Happened to the Human Race?*, it was a situation where "one era is quite certain intellectually and emotionally about what is acceptable...yet another era decides that these 'certainties' are unacceptable and puts another set of values into practice. On a humanistic base, people drift along from generation to generation, and the morally unthinkable becomes thinkable as the years move on." Biblical Christians can clearly see this happening in our day in the societal shift in attitude toward gay marriage and homosexuality in general. Schaeffer and Koop went on,

"By 'humanistic base' we mean the fundamental idea that men and women can begin from themselves and derive the standards by which to judge all matters...There are for such people no fixed standards of behavior, no standards that cannot be eroded or replaced by what seems necessary, expedient, or even fashionable."[65]

What happened with the Hitler Youth was, of course, *accelerated*—because all other ideas had been *removed* from consideration. It was the principle of "prima facie" at work: What is espoused and repeated without opposition will become accepted as fact. It was Hitler's *modus operandi*. "Make the lie big," he said, "make it simple, keep saying it, and eventually they will believe it."[66]

Yet what is happening in our current and expanding Western culture is that today's humanist proponents have a good many adherents who are mindlessly "goose-stepping" to the same beat. The educational system—together with swiftly-moving advances in technology, including information technology—have set the stage for the

---

[65] Francis A. Schaeffer and Dr. C. Everett Koop, Whatever Happened to the Human Race?, Revised Edition, (Wheaton, IL: Crossway Books, 1983) pp.16-17
[66] Adolf Hitler. BrainyQuote.com, Xplore Inc, 2012. http://www.brainyquote.com/quotes/quotes/a/adolfhitle378177.html

precipitous erasure of long-standing Bible-based moral teachings and the advent of a godless moral atmosphere that includes a growing "culture of death,"[67] as it has been called.

Transience and Acceleration—the Disorienting Nature of "Future Shock"

Schaeffer and Koop noted the acceleration of the change of moral ideas in our modern time:

> "Perhaps the most striking and unusual feature of our moment of history is the speed with which eras change…what was unthinkable in the sixties [they wrote in 1979] is no longer unthinkable. The ease and speed of communication has been a factor in this."

They said, rather prophetically (emphasis mine):

---

[67] The term, "culture of death" was used twelve times in the *Evangelium vitae*, published by Pope John Paul II in March of 1995. http://www.vatican.va/holy_father/john_paul_ii/encyclicals/documents/ hf_jp-ii_enc_25031995_evangelium-vitae_en.html. The term has been used in recent years to describe the growing cultural acceptability of abortion, euthanasia, physician-assisted suicide and other related doctrines (philosophies) which "violate…the integrity of the human person" and "insult human dignity."

"The thinkables of the eighties and nineties will certainly include things which most people today find unthinkable and immoral, even unimaginable and too extreme to suggest. Yet—*since they do not have some overriding principle that takes them beyond relativistic thinking*—when these become thinkable and acceptable in the eighties and nineties, most people will not even remember that they were unthinkable in the seventies. They will slide into each new thinkable without a jolt."[68]

It has been noted that "what we regard as thinkable and unthinkable about how we treat human life has changed drastically in the West. For centuries Western culture has regarded human life and the quality of the life of the individual as special. It has been common to speak of 'the sanctity of human life.'"[69] It seems that the centuries-long ideal has been turned on its ear in a very short time indeed.

This is happening not only due to the propagation of humanistic philosophies and a socialistic agenda in the

---

[68] Schaeffer/Koop, p.17
[69] Ibid.

educational institutions of the West—although those are essential factors of cause-and-effect—but also, as has been suggested, to the acceleration of the "ease and speed of communication" in our society. Since this was suggested in the 1970's the speed of such change has been astounding. This alone has loosed our society-at-large from previously long-held religious moorings. The effect of "transience" or *change* in our society, brought about by technological advances and the advanced speed of communicating those changes, is disorienting enough to make people feel lost and bewildered *in their own culture*. This is because there is no permanence to our culture anymore. Traditions have fallen to the onslaught of transience.

Alvin Toffler brought this out vividly in his incredibly insightful book, *Future Shock*. Toffler indicated how sudden change is disorienting—as we can see in the case of "culture shock" when someone travels to foreign soil. A traveler may find themselves "in a place where yes may mean no, where a 'fixed price' is negotiable, where to be kept waiting in an outer office is no cause for insult, where laughter may signify anger." Toffler brings to light the similar and compounded effects of when *the future* is superimposed on the present not merely through "change"—but through tremendous changes that are hitting our entire society at an *accelerated pace*. We are thrust into a new society so quickly we cannot adjust—and then major change hits us again. To a child—especially a child growing up without any strong biblical traditions in his or her daily diet—*the only thing that seems constant IS change*. There is no chance for long-held societal mores to be inculcated into their lives for it seems there are none of which to grasp hold. It is not "culture shock"—it is "future shock." As Toffler said, "The malaise, mass neurosis, irrationality, and free-floating violence already apparent in contemporary life are merely a foretaste of what may lie ahead...future shock is a phenomenon, a product of the greatly accelerated rate of change in society. It arises from the imposition of a new culture on an old one. It is culture shock in one's own society."[70] The "feeling of impermanence"[71] is fed and intensified by living in a state of constant "transience"—a state where everything is constantly changing—and by the humanistic/evolutionary teaching that man is merely a product of time and chance.

---

[70] Alvin Toffler, Future Shock (New York, NY: Bantam, 1971), pp.10-11
[71] Ibid., p.45

These are the actualities of our current culture—and they are synergistic in their promotion of the concept that human life is *cheap, expendable* for the most insignificant of reasons, and not worth the expense of maintaining should that life become "devoid of value."

Chapter Four

Recent Changes in the View of the
Sanctity of Human Life

"[Often] ethics prescribes higher standards of behavior than does the law, and occasionally ethics requires that physicians disobey laws that demand unethical behavior.... The WMA ensures that its ethical policy statements reflect a consensus by requiring a 75% vote in favor of any new or revised policy at its annual Assembly.... It is generally accepted that physicians may in exceptional situations have to place the interests of others above those of the patient."

Medical Ethics Manual, 3rd Edition 2015
World Medical Association

W e will start this discussion with a quote: "The Hippocratic Oath, which goes back more than two thousand years, has been traditionally taken by graduates of American medical schools at the time of their commencement. The Declaration of Geneva (adopted in September 1948 by the General Assembly of the World Medical Association and closely modeled on the Hippocratic Oath) became used as the graduation oath of more and more medical schools. It includes: 'I will maintain the utmost respect for human life from the time of conception.'"[72] This is the basic precept that has been traditionally adhered to and believed in Western society up until the last several decades.

It is interesting to note that many medical schools who have adopted the Declaration of Geneva oath have dropped the clause "from the moment of conception."[73] Some, such as Albany Medical College, have replaced "from the moment of conception" with "even under threat."[74]

As Drs. Schaeffer and Koop opined, "Judeo-Christian teaching...[laid] a foundation for a high view of human life

---

[72] Schaeffer/Koop, p.17
[73] Ibid., pp.17; 20
[74] As given at the 2009 commencement exercise in Albany, NY

as unique—to be protected and loved—because each individual is created in the image of God. This stands in great contrast to...[ancient] Roman culture. The Roman world practiced both abortion and infanticide, while Christian societies have considered abortion and infanticide to be murder." They went on, "Until recently...with some notable and sorry exceptions, human beings have generally been regarded as special, unique, and nonexpendable. But *in one short generation* [during the time of Roe v. Wade] we have moved from a generally high view of life to a very low one."[75]

To anyone who would care to look with any objectivity, our societal mores regarding the preciousness and sacredness of human life have clearly deteriorated since even the time of that writing. I believe this is because of the humanistic idealism that has pervaded most of the institutions of learning and government in Western culture, including the United States. This idealism is pervasive in the majority of media outlets in this country as well. While I cannot cite a source for that last statement—other than

---

[75] Ibid., p.20

some radio talk-show hosts—one can simply notice the ubiquitous biases in both the reporting and the rhetoric.

Fortunately a large percentage of our U.S. population has had enough teaching—moral teaching stemming from the Scriptures—lingering as a vestige in our society, to give the population at large a slightly conservative bent (albeit, this is deteriorating at an alarming pace). This is reflected in some recent polling data by the Gallup organization. Gallup related in a May 2011 article that "Gallup's 2011 *Values and Beliefs Survey*, conducted May 5-8, finds...public agreement about the morality of abortion. Just over half of Americans, 51%, believe abortion is 'morally wrong,' while 39% say it is 'morally acceptable.' Americans' views on this have been fairly steady since 2002, except for 2006, when they were evenly divided."[76] Since 2011/2012, when this book was first written as a theological paper, there has continued to be a shift to the left on issues of morality, and that shift has accelerated. The 2015 Gallup *Values and Beliefs Survey* still showed only 45% of the American population polled believed abortion to be "morally acceptable." The same number,

---

[76]   http://www.gallup.com/poll/147734/Americans-Split-Along-Pro-Choice-Pro-Life-Lines.aspx Retrieved 1/16/12

45% said they believed abortion to be morally wrong—this is a decided shift to the left from the 2011 polling data. This was reported in an online report entitled *Americans Continue to Shift Left on Key Moral Issues.*[77] Americans are holding somewhat to long-instilled societal moral values despite the near constant barrage of negative comments in the media and by the political left regarding the "right to life" community. Yet the onslaught of the barrage *is* having its effect—seemingly at an increased rate. The shift in the last four years is disturbing, even while it may be expected. This is shades of Toffler's "transience and acceleration."

Reported polling data from Gallup in 2001 indicated a fair amount of conservative value relative to the abortion issue throughout the years from 1975 (two years after Roe v. Wade) up to the 2011 poll. When asked the question, "Do you think abortions should be legal under any circumstances, legal only under certain circumstances, or illegal in all circumstances?" the majority of respondents have consistently felt that it should be legal only "under certain circumstances" with lower and fairly-closely-

---

[77]   http://www.gallup.com/poll/183413/americans-continue-shift-left-key-moral-issues.aspx, accessed October 30, 2016

matched responses for "legal under any" and "illegal in all" circumstances. For example, the 1975 data indicate 54% of respondents felt it should be legal only under certain circumstances while 22% felt it should be illegal in all circumstances, and 21% legal under any circumstances. The 2011 data was not far off with 50% responding "legal under certain," 22% "illegal in all," and 27% responding "legal under any."

Given the general trend toward a more liberal stance, the overall conservative bent was comforting. However, the direction is not encouraging—especially when there is a pronounced trend toward socialized medicine in the current administration in Washington and when media outlets continually spout that mantra as well.

A reasonable speculation would be that "illegal in all" circumstances would have generated the highest percentage in the 1940s or 50s but, as no polling data exists for those decades, it remains merely speculation. It is speculation, however, that is based on other, very apparent evidences of a deeper moral fiber present in American society prior to the 1960s.

The Humanist Mantra

When I speak of "the mantra" here, I refer to the myriad utterances that have their base in the philosophical underpinnings that are so intertwined in the worldview of left-leaning governmental officials and educational elites that they cannot help but be expressed when they or their (often mindless) adherents speak.

The mantra was codified by John Dewey and others in the famed Humanist Manifesto of 1933, and received further elaboration in the 1973 version (Humanist Manifesto II), and later in the 2003 version. One signer of all three documents, Lester Mondale, was the older half-brother of former U.S. Vice-President Walter Mondale.[78]

The Humanist Manifestos I, II and III have a socialist/anti-God base; and stand against moral values that derive their base from the Bible or any moral code seen as coming from a supernatural source. In other words, in their view, all morality is derived from man, and not God—and

---

[78] When Walter Mondale was a U.S. Senator he addressed the Fifth *International Humanist and Ethical Union World Congress* held in Boston in 1970. See http://philosopedia.org/index.php/Lester_Mondale

is therefore relativistic and situational. Here are some quotes from the first Manifesto:[79]

- Religious humanists regard the universe as self-existing and not created. [Translation: there is no Creator—and therefore no "Judge."]

- Holding an organic view of life, humanists find that the traditional dualism of mind and body must be rejected. [Translation: We are just animals—products of natural evolution; there is no "soul."]

- Humanism asserts that the nature of the universe depicted by modern science makes unacceptable any supernatural or cosmic guarantees of human values...Religion must formulate its hopes and plans in the light of the scientific spirit and method.

---

[79]

http://www.americanhumanist.org/Who_We_Are/About_Humanism/Humanist_Manifesto_I

[Translation: we don't receive our values from any God.]

- We are convinced that the time has passed for theism. [Translation: Bible-believing churches should be done away with.]

- Certainly religious institutions, their ritualistic forms, ecclesiastical methods, and communal activities must be reconstituted as rapidly as experience allows, in order to function effectively in the modern world. [Translation: All churches should become Unitarian humanistic churches—the sooner the better.]

- The humanists are firmly convinced that existing acquisitive and profit-motivated society has shown itself to be inadequate and that a radical change in methods, controls, and motives must be instituted. A socialized and cooperative economic order must be established to the end that the equitable distribution of the means of life be possible. The goal of humanism is a free and universal society in which people voluntarily and intelligently cooperate for the common good. Humanists demand a shared life in a shared world. [Translation: Capitalism is evil because we say so, and socialism will usher in Utopia.]

Through this we can see what John Dewey thought as he was working out his thoughts on public education as a tool for "social reform" in America. The Humanist Manifesto II was even more direct[80]:

- Traditional moral codes and newer irrational cults both fail to meet the pressing needs of today and tomorrow. False "theologies of hope" and messianic ideologies, substituting new dogmas for old, cannot cope with existing world realities. [Translation:

80

http://www.americanhumanist.org/Who_We_Are/About_Humanism/Humanist_Manifesto_II

Theology is bankrupt and cannot meet human needs.]

• Traditional dogmatic or authoritarian religions that place revelation, God, ritual, or creed above human needs and experience do a disservice to the human species. Any account of nature should pass the tests of scientific evidence; in our judgment, the dogmas and myths of traditional religions do not do so…We find insufficient evidence for belief in the existence of a supernatural…As nontheists, we begin with humans not God, nature not deity. [Translation: Religion is repressive and harmful. Even though evolution does not pass scientific scrutiny, we believe that creationism must—just don't call us on our hypocrisy!]

• Humans are responsible for what we are or will become. No deity will save us; we must save ourselves. [No translation needed.]

- Promises of immortal salvation or fear of eternal damnation are both illusory and harmful. Traditional religions…[are] obstacles to human progress. [No translation needed.]

- We affirm that moral values derive their source from human experience. Ethics is autonomous and situational needing no theological or ideological sanction. [Translation: We make up our own morals based on what we think is best for the situation. Keep your Bible out of my business!]

- We reject all religious, ideological, or moral codes that denigrate the individual, suppress freedom… [They state this after affirming individual human dignity—yet the individual is not important to the humanist, rather the society as a whole is what must be served. It is apparent they feel that "moral codes" suppress freedom.]

- In the area of sexuality, we believe that intolerant attitudes, often cultivated by orthodox religions and puritanical cultures, unduly repress sexual conduct. The right to birth control, abortion, and divorce should be recognized. [Note: *They* decide what "unduly" means.]

- To enhance freedom and dignity the individual must experience a full range of civil liberties...It also includes a recognition of an individual's right to die with dignity, euthanasia, and the right to suicide.[81] [Note the code words, "die with dignity."]

- We deplore the division of humankind on nationalistic grounds. We

---

[81] It should be noted that their constant use of terms similar to "death with dignity" all stems from the idea promoted that life "devoid of value" is a life that should not continue. The problem is compounded in that they want to set the social agenda as to what constitutes a life devoid of value.

have reached a turning point in human history where the best option is to transcend the limits of national sovereignty and to move toward the building of a world community in which all sectors of the human family can participate. Thus we look to the development of a system of world law and a world order based upon transnational federal government. [Translation: One World Government.]

• World poverty must cease. Hence extreme disproportions in wealth, income, and economic growth should be reduced on a worldwide basis. [Translation: Disproportions in wealth and income reduced equals socialism. They believe socialism's "redistribution of wealth" will "end poverty," even though every time it has been tried it *produces* poverty!]

• We would resist any moves to censor basic scientific research on

85

moral, political, or social grounds. [Translation: Research on embryonic stem cells.]

Such statements made in isolation would not be cause for concern—yet this is hardly being done in a corner. We hear the mantra—perhaps in differing words, but in matching ideologies— from both the political left and from the media. Also, the signers of the Manifestos are well known elitists.

The impressive list of signers includes: John Dewey (father of American Progressive Education and the American Public School System), R. Lester Mondale (brother to former Vice-President Mondale), Isaac Asimov (noted author), Francis Crick (co-discoverer of DNA and Nobel Prize Laureate), Sidney H. Scheuer (onetime Chairman of the National Committee for an Effective Congress), B.F. Skinner (noted Behavioral Scientist, former Professor of Psychology at Harvard University, and author of *Beyond Freedom and Dignity*), John Anton (famed Professor at Emory University), Betty Friedan (Founder, National Organization of Women), Irving Horowitz (Editor, Society Magazine), Sir_Julian Huxley (former head, UNESCO, Great Britain), as well as a very long list of other senior professors, corporate presidents, journalists, scientists, teachers, executives, authors, ministers, poets and union directors from across the world.

Many of the signers are educators at the highest levels from major universities across the globe. They are training our population—including *our* school teachers, journalists, government leaders and medical professionals.

With the mantra being proclaimed in universities across the land, on airwaves, and in political speeches, it will inevitably have its desired effect. Hitler's idea worked for him: "Make the lie big, make it simple, keep saying it, and eventually they will believe it." Schaeffer bolsters this point: "By constant repetition, the idea that man is nothing more than a machine has captured the popular mind. This idea keeps being presented year after year in the schools and in the media, however unfounded and unproven the hypothesis. Gradually, after being generally unquestioned, it is blindly accepted."[82] It is the prima facie principle at work. This is why we must *counter* the prima facie voices with our own voice! More of this will be discussed in the next chapter.

---

[82] Schaeffer/Koop, p.21

I should not fail to mention that, with the shifting of Western thought by means of the incessant mantra and with biblical foundations removed from consideration, the debate becomes emotional. Nietzsche claimed that "both Christian theology and Christian morality have badly damaged human beings, and human well-being therefore requires the total rejection of Christianity."[83] In our increasingly secularized society, morality is largely viewed through emotional eyes and is not anchored to biblical roots. One author, Michael J. Hyde, was compelled to write *The Call of Conscience* after watching his father's health deteriorate following kidney failure. The author opined what it must be like and suggested one thought that might be going through the heads of the terminally-ill: "Is modern medicine prolonging my living or my dying?" Hyde's book dealt with the philosophical constructs, was emotionally-driven (in my opinion), and quotes Nietzsche extensively.[84]

Such books are numerous—and such opinions are nearly overwhelming in that they constitute the majority opinion in print. The sounding of a Christian perspective,

---

[83] David Gushee, The Sacredness of Human Life (Grand Rapids, MI: Eerdmans, 2013), p.284

[84] Michael J. Hyde, The Call of Conscience (Columbia, SC: University of South Carolina Press, 2001), p.119

one which puts forth biblical absolutes as the foundation of our decisions, is essential. Hyde's book appealed to society's conscience. Yet what of the conscience of a nation that has allowed the legal abortion of nearly 59 million babies since Roe v. Wade[85] and a number of infants to starve to death over perceived "quality of life" issues decided by others?

It was a rare thing indeed when Ronald Reagan, as a sitting President of the United States wrote *Abortion and the Conscience of a Nation* near the middle of his first term. In it, he strongly condemned the philosophical underpinnings of the abortion issue as well as the arguments of those pushing the message of abortion-on-demand. He indicated that medical infanticide is abortion's logical consequence. He said, "Regrettably, we live at a time when some persons do not value all human life. They want to pick and choose which individuals have value....In other words, 'quality control'...." He exposed a "quality of life" ethic in opposition to a "sanctity of life" ethic.[86] Unfortunately, his words were overridden by the mantra.

---

[85] http://www.nrlc.org/uploads/factsheets/FS01AbortionintheUS.pdf, Accessed December 15, 2016.
[86] Ronald Reagan, Abortion and the Conscience of a Nation (Nashville, TN: Thomas Nelson Publishers, 1984), pp.24,25,31

He supported the Respect Human Life Act (S. 467, 1983)[87] which was written "to protect innocent human life, both before and after birth." That Act died in Congress.

Alas, with such overpowering voices calling for "the destruction of life [supposedly] devoid of value"[88] it is more critical than ever that the voices of godly leaders be lifted up like a trumpet.

---

[87] S. 467 — 98th Congress: Respect Human Life Act of 1983." www.GovTrack.us. 1983. December 15, 2016 <https://www.govtrack.us/congress/bills/98/s467>
[88] See footnote on page 22, and addition discussion in Chapter Six regarding this term.

Chapter Five

Sounding Out

CR

"For every one pupil who needs to be guarded from a weak excess of sensibility there are three who need to be awakened from the slumber of cold vulgarity. The task of the modern educator is not to cut down jungles but to irrigate deserts. The right defense against false sentiments is to inculcate just sentiments. By starving the sensibility of our pupils we only make them easier prey to the propagandist when he comes."

C.S. Lewis, 1944

I t is imperative that we ministers of the Gospel of Jesus Christ raise our voices counter to the prima facie voices that prevail in our day. It is also imperative that Christian parents raise their voices and stand with the pulpit on these issues—and that they are not silent in the home. Parents must diligently teach godly principles in the home and in the daily conduct of life (Deuteronomy 6:1-9). If the ubiquitous voices of the humanistic worldview go unchallenged, those voices will be blindly accepted. While I understand that we counter many things in our culture I also recognize that our awareness and understanding of the issues at hand needs to be generally elevated if we are to counter the culture of death being foisted upon our society.

What was *discussed* in medical journals and in classrooms in the seventies is being *implemented* in more and more venues across our Western society. Some Christian medical professionals may not be aware that they have been influenced. Joseph Fletcher, a major promoter of situational ethics, said this in 1973 in an article regarding "death with dignity" in the American Journal of Nursing:

"It is ridiculous to give ethical approval
to the positive ending of sub-human life in
utero as we do in therapeutic abortions for

reasons of mercy and compassion but refuse to approve of positively ending a sub-human life in extremis. If we are morally obligated to put an end to a pregnancy when an amniocentesis reveals a terribly defective fetus, we are equally obliged to put an end to a patient's hopeless misery when a brain scan reveals that a patient with cancer has advanced brain metastases."[89]

Here he argued several things that must be countered from a biblical perspective:

1.   A baby *in utero* is <u>not</u> sub-human life but is precious human life! Psalm 139 gives us the marvelous perspective that we are fearfully and wonderfully made in the womb. The Psalm is rich with personal pronouns—telling us that baby in the Psalmist's mother's womb was none other than HIM (the Psalmist), and not some impersonal mass of tissue: "Thou hast covered *me* in *my* mother's womb (v. 13); Thine eyes did see *my* substance, yet being unperfect" (v. 16).

---

[89] Joseph Fletcher, Ethics and Euthanasia, American Journal of Nursing 73:670 (1973) as cited in Schaeffer/Koop, p.99

2.   In this scenario, a doctor ordered (likely without much discussion of the process—or the *purpose*) an amniocentesis. This is a common procedure—yet most pregnant women (and their spouses) are not told why. The reason for an amniocentesis is primarily to look at the amniotic fluid for any signs that a baby has a birth defect such as Down syndrome.[90] One online medical encyclopedia did give this as a precaution: "The serious emotional and ethical dilemmas that adverse test results can bring must also be considered."[91] Indeed, a negative test result brings incredible pressure upon a couple to abort their baby—and counsel is often given to abort, as Fletcher said, "for reasons of mercy and compassion"— or as Bing and Hoche said in their pivotal book of the 1920's, because the life of a Down syndrome child is, in their view, "devoid of value." For this reason, many Christian pro-life advocates recommend *against* having an amniocentesis performed. I stand with them.

3.   Fletcher argues that one is morally obliged to end a cancer patient's life prematurely—as one

---

[90] http://www.surgeryencyclopedia.com/A-Ce/Amniocentesis.html
[91] Ibid.

would put a horse out of its misery—claiming that the cancer patient is now, quite literally, "sub-human." It is the argument that the person's life is devoid of value. Yet there IS value, intrinsic value, to all human life. VanDrunen, in his *Bioethics and the Christian Life*, argues that the dying and those who are close to them benefit greatly from ongoing community with one another—and much can be gained from close interaction during their last days.[92]

Fletcher is not a lone voice in sounding out this type of reasoning. A major bioethics work published in 1985 by Peter Singer and Helga Kuhse through Oxford University Press, *Should the Baby Live? The Problem of Handicapped Infants*, is still widely referenced in medical ethics publications today. In fact, it was referenced in an early 2012 publication of the *Journal of Medical Ethics* which included a paper entitled *"After-birth abortion: why should the baby live?"* wherein the authors argued that because abortion is deemed morally acceptable by society [rather glossing over the strong segment of our society that disagrees], and whereas "the newborn and the fetus are

---

[92] VanDrunen, pp. 183-184

morally equivalent," it is morally acceptable to kill a newborn.[93,94]

The paper argues in a rather circular fashion that "both a fetus and a newborn certainly are human beings and potential persons, but neither is a 'person' in the sense of 'subject to moral right to life'. We take 'person' to mean an individual who is capable of attributing to her own existence some (at least) basic value such that being deprived of this existence represents a loss to her. This means that [are you ready for this?] many non-human animals and mentally retarded human individuals are persons, but that all individuals who are not in the condition of attributing any value to their own existence are not persons. Merely being human is not in itself a reason for ascribing someone a right to life."[95]

Here the authors actually seem to be arguing that your cognizant family pet may be a "person" who has an inherent "right to life," but that neither a newborn baby nor

---

[93] http://www.telegraph.co.uk/health/healthnews/9113394/Killing-babies-no-different-from-abortion-experts-say.html, Retrieved March 3, 2012
[94] http://jme.bmj.com/content/early/2012/02/22/medethics-2011-100411.full.pdf+html, Retrieved March 3, 2012
[95] Ibid, p.2

a comatose adult are a "person" with an inherent "right to life."

Unfortunately, it is this type of writing that makes it *frequently* into the medical and nursing journals to which our medical professionals regularly subscribe. We would be foolish to think that such morally bankrupt philosophies are not affecting the medical community that we and our congregants interact with on a routine basis. Many people in our congregations are, in fact, members of the healthcare community and are subject to these frequent pourings-forth from among their peers. Many among them who are strong biblical Christians will see these articles for what they are—others may be influenced without even realizing that what they are reading on their lunch break is contrary to biblical truth. They need to hear the biblical view preached and taught.

It is equally important for the minister or counselor to become knowledgeable concerning other issues that are made more complicated by advances in medical technology. We shall consider some of these in the next chapter.

Chapter Six

Complex Bioethical Issues

"Advances in medical science and technology raise new ethical issues that cannot be answered by traditional medical ethics. Assisted reproduction, genetics, health informatics and life-extending and enhancing technologies... have great potential for benefiting patients but also potential harm depending on how they are put into practice....

Given the inherent unpredictability of the future, medical ethics needs to be flexible and open to change and adjustment, as indeed it has been for some time now."

Medical Ethics Manual, 3rd Edition 2015
World Medical Association

Infertility Treatments

Great strides have been made in the treatment of infertility—and it is naturally appealing to a childless couple to consider some medical means of increasing their chances of having a child. Yet the industry of infertility treatment raises several bioethical questions. We shall only deal with those that are pertinent to sanctity of life issues, although other bioethical questions may be raised as well.

Some infertility treatments include the creation of several human embryos (unique persons in a biblical sense, even if not in the sense of the U.S. Constitution as currently viewed since Roe v. Wade), typically through the means of in vitro fertilization. Not all of these embryos are brought to birth: some are frozen using cryogenic technology. What is to become of these people-in-embryo?

In my opinion, it would be unethical for a Christian to use an infertility treatment that calls for the potential of creating multiple embryos when the aim is to have a single child. Additionally, some infertility treatments often result in multiple babies competing, quite unnaturally, inside a mother's womb for the nutrients needed to sustain life and growth. In several known cases of quintuplets and other

101

large progenies of children, the sacrifice (abortion) of some children to increase the chance of survival of others is sometimes indicated by the medical community as "necessary" if any of the children are to survive. While this is true, the situation should never have been created.

Prospective Christian parents should be aware that their actions in trying to have a family may result in the unnatural creation of a situation where children need to die for the saving of other children—and that they should not engage in such actions in keeping with the biblical moral injunctions related to the sanctity of human life.

Organ Transplantation

I shall not deal here with the morality of whether it is or is not right to donate body organs, such as eyes, hearts, lungs, etc. after death or donations during the course of your life such as being a bone-marrow or kidney donor. On a personal level, I do not see a valid biblical or moral reason not to donate (or receive) such organs. Yet organ transplantation can indeed create some bioethical issues— or at least highlight some underlying bioethical sentiments that are contrary to the Scriptures.

It is amazing that mankind can now take the donated heart out of a recently deceased auto accident victim and place that heart into another human whose heart has ceased to function properly—and give that person a new lease on life with a new heart. It is amazing that a child whose kidneys have ceased to function can receive the kidney (or kidneys) of a donor, and live a normal life.

Nonetheless—as wonderful as this is to the recipient and their family—there is usually a greater need than supply. How are decisions made as to who gets a kidney, and who does not? Of course, compatibility between the donor and the recipient is an issue with many transplants (such as kidneys)—yet beyond the compatibility issue lies another issue. Is an older person denied a life-saving transplant just because they are 70—even if they are otherwise in good health and making a meaningful and positive impact on their community? Is a child denied because they have some other "defect," and are therefore deemed to have a life that is, at least somewhat, "devoid of value." "Surely not!" you might say. Yet this IS the case in many places.

In a January 18, 2012 Associated Press story it was reported that "the parents of a three-year-old New Jersey girl was [sic] denied a needed kidney transplant because of her 'mental disabilities.'"[96] Chrissy Rivera, the child's mother, stated that "a doctor at The Children's Hospital of Philadelphia told her and her husband that their daughter would not be eligible for a transplant because of her [daughter's] mental condition."[97] Their daughter, Amelia, was born with Wolf-Hirschhorn syndrome, a rare genetic defect which causes varying degrees of mental retardation as well as some other issues. The mother's story was also relayed on a website dedicated to the syndrome. She quotes the doctor, "No. She is not eligible because of her quality of life; Because [sic] of her mental delays."[98]

While a child with Wolf-Hirschhorn syndrome can have other physical issues, such as heart defects, that could make a transplant much riskier, there was no evidence presented that this was the reason for the denial. The reason given, according to the sources cited, was that the child's "quality of life" and her "mental delays" were the deciding factors. The quality of life argument does not hold water

[96]http://hosted.ap.org/dynamic/stories/U/US_DISABLED_CHILD_TR ANSPLANT?SITE=AP&SECTION=HOME&TEMPLATE=DEFAUL T Retrieved January 19, 2012
[97] Ibid.
[98] http://www.wolfhirschhorn.org/2012/01/amelia/brick-walls/ Retrieved January 19, 2012

because God, the Author of life, grants many wonderful blessings to people with a variety of illnesses and handicaps—and to their families *through* them; and the Author of life upholds the sanctity of human life through His Word, including the basic commandment, "thou shalt not kill (murder)." The doctor's statement indicates a worldview that does not allow for those with mental disabilities to lead fulfilling, meaningful lives. This is simply not the case—as myriad testimonials would confirm.[99] While the hospital distanced itself from the opinion of the doctor when this became a national news story, the doctor's opinion represents a Kantian/Hegelian worldview in which all ethical matters are situational and where "absolutes," such as the absolute sanctity of human life, are passé.

What if this child were a future Temple Grandin or Albert Einstein? We all know who Einstein was, but many do not know that he was a late talker (he did not begin speaking until age 4).[100] Temple Grandin was and is autistic. She holds a PhD in Animal Science and is a

---

[99] For example, See: http://www.wolfhirschhorn.org/our-stories/
[100] Thomas Sowell, The Einstein Syndrome: Bright Children Who Talk Late (New York, NY: Basic Books, 2001)

professor of Animal Science at Colorado State University and a world-renowned autism spokesperson (she has been called "The Voice of Autism") as well as a consultant to the livestock industry on animal behavior.

Grandin is a very in-demand speaker at conferences in a variety of fields, the author of several books, and an inventor and designer of facilities in at least three continents. In 2010, *Time Magazine* named her one of the 100 most influential people who affect our world.[101,102] She once said, "If I could snap my fingers and be non-autistic, I would not...Autism is part of who I am."[103] Of course, one does not need to be an Einstein or a Temple Grandin to be an example of a child with perceived impairments or disabilities who has or can have a quality life. Every human life is precious.

Another bioethical issue arises from the advance of organ transplantation: namely, the *pressure* placed upon families (and doctors and medical institutions) to harvest organs from victims of serious injury and others. Medical

---

[101] http://grandin.com/temple.html, accessed October 31, 2016

[102] http://content.time.com/time/specials/packages/article/0,28804,1984 685_1984949_1985222,00.html, accessed October 31, 2016

[103] http://www.newyorker.com/magazine/1993/12/27/anthropologist-mars, accessed October 31, 2016

institutions have financial pressure placed upon them to approach families of individuals who are potential "donors" of organs that are wanted for patients elsewhere.

As a pastor who has assisted families in such crisis situations, I have seen—firsthand—the pressure placed by doctors upon families to remove life support even *before* it was clear there was no medical intervention that could save the person's life. This does not happen everywhere, but it happens more often than one might think.

I had one instance where the doctor told the family of a man that "the next 24 to 48 hours will be critical" in determining whether the man could be saved. We expected to wait the 24 to 48 hours as we prayed, but when the man's wife left the room, the doctor came to me quickly and said "I really see no hope," and counselled me to counsel the family to "let him go." They had already put pressure on the family to remove him from a breathing machine and let him pass.

When I told the doctor that I had discussed it with the wife and we chose to pray and believe, he became angry. He told the wife over the next day that her husband would never open his eyes again—or if he did he would never speak, swallow, move his arms, or walk. She was urged all the next day to remove him from life-support and to consider organ donation. She refused. The next day her husband opened his eyes and responded to questions. The following day he was moving his limbs. That week he was talking normally and eating—and several weeks later I saw him walk into our church for service.

Potential organ donations can lead to unwarranted pressure to suspend life-saving measures because of a perceived "quality of life" issue should their patient survive. This sentiment is rooted in a secular humanist worldview that does not value every human life. Christian families and pastors must be aware of these pressures *before* they face them. Christian healthcare workers need to be aware that their industry is increasingly subscribing to a secular worldview regarding human life. We must not only be and remain aware—we must stand for a biblical view in a growing sea of contrary opinion. There may be times when this stand will cost us.

Stem Cell Research and Therapy Using Human Embryos

Stem cells are a hot topic in the field of medical research. The topic is new enough that there is not even an entry for "stem cell" in my 1997 edition *Webster's Encyclopedic Unabridged Dictionary of the English Language*. It is also among the most controversial areas of medical research today due, in part, to pro-choice groups pushing Federal funding for research using stem cells derived from human embryos.

First, it would be beneficial for us to define what a stem cell is, and why it is important to medical research. A stem cell is "an unspecialized cell capable of perpetuating itself through cell division and having the potential to give rise to differentiated cells with specialized functions."[104] In other words, they are cells that can potentially turn into any kind of specialized cell.

In terms of medical possibilities, the potential appears staggering at first glance (and in some respects, it *is*). Then, however, come the pesky details. Since stem cell research is advancing on various fronts at the present time, and since

---

[104] http://www.merriam-webster.com/dictionary/stem%20cell, Accessed November 1, 2016

this author is not an expert on the subject, we cannot exhaust this topic here. We can only hope to look at some of the prevailing science, identify points and counterpoints often used in the stem cell debate, examine some of the evidence, and then subject the whole thing to the scrutiny of the Word of God. Ultimately, we need to see how this affects people on a personal level in terms of *decisions* we might be asked to make relative to healthcare.

Not all stem cells available for research and potential therapy are derived from human embryos. I should mention at the onset that, as stated earlier in this book, Christians must view a human embryo as fully human from the moment of conception. The biblical evidence for this view is insurmountable as discussed in some detail in Chapter 2.

With the advent of stem cell research, abortion advocates (this typically means advocates for abortion-on-demand) seized the opportunity to make abortion-on-demand as attractive as possible both on a financial level and a sympathetic level. If stem cells could be cultured and turned into replacement organs—literally growing a human heart, for example, in a laboratory setting, and then placing that heart into someone who needs a heart transplant—that would be an incredible breakthrough. This is one example of the general thrust of the technology. As embryos are rich in stem cells as compared to matured humans, this suddenly made human embryos a marketable commodity—and the pro-abortion crowd seized the moment with an appeal to patients everywhere.

This, of course, is an emotion-packed appeal to people who have had a long-standing Judeo-Christian ethic removed from their everyday thinking by the aforementioned "mantra"—and who are now facing a life-threatening disease or condition that embryonic stem cell research advocates claim could be healed if research were not held up by those moralistic Neanderthals who keep getting in the way.

In dealing with this issue, I should point out that stem cell research is being conducted with stem cells from embryos, from placental tissue (also rich in stem cells), and from adult human tissues—and that the most promising research and achievements have been from the use of adult stem cells. Part of this is, admittedly, due to the fact that embryonic stem cell research has been battled, in terms of getting government funding, by those on the religious right who have objected on the grounds that such research would tend to make human embryos an exploitable commodity for financial reasons (which is exactly true), and on the grounds that a human embryo is, in fact, a human life. Another major reason is simply that there are fewer problems experienced with adult stem cells for functional reasons that will be identified below.

In 1996, the U.S. Congress passed legislation that made it illegal for federal funds to be used to fund research in which human embryos would be either created or destroyed. The debate, in the meanwhile, continued, with decisions within the Bush administration (2001) allowing for limited research involving 64 "existing lines" of embryonic stem cells (Bush later rescinded the funding). In 2009 the Obama administration—via executive order— lifted restrictions on embryonic stem cell research under certain conditions, and then, in January 2013, the U.S. Supreme Court lifted the restrictions altogether by refusing to hear an appeal to rescind the Obama executive order of 2009.[105,106] One writer said that, "Obama reasoned that research on stem cell lines from embryos created through in

---

[105] http://www.cnn.com/2013/01/07/justice/stem-cell-appeal/, Accessed November 7, 2016.
[106] http://usnews.nbcnews.com/_news/2013/01/07/16395707-supreme-court-lets-embryonic-stem-cell-research-go-forward?lite, Accessed November 7, 2016.

vitro fertilization was not ethically problematic."[107] So now we have our taxes at work to fund research using stem cells from human embryos created in vitro.

Nonetheless, embryonic stem cell research appears to carry with it several problems that adult stem cells do not have—and adult stem cell research is already paying dividends. These are dividends that appear to be unlikely with embryonic stem cells. While stem cells from embryos are *pluripotent*, that is, they can be become all cell types in the human body, they are also believed to raise a great many significant hurdles to actual use in humans due to the fact that tissue derived from embryonic stem cells faces rejection once implanted into a recipient and will require anti-rejection drugs that carry their own serious risk factors. Adult stem cells derived from patients can be used to create tissues that will not be rejected when implanted. Major strides have already been made.[108]

The question ought to be asked—and has been—as to why the Obama administration and others pushed for greater funding for the problem-ridden and unpromising

---

[107] Ibid.
[108] https://stemcells.nih.gov/info/basics/5.htm, Accessed November 7, 2016.

embryonic stem cell research efforts, but are not at all interested in the advancement of adult stem cell research. To me the answer is obvious: it lies in ideology. The ideology of the left is based on secular humanistic philosophy and not at all upon the Judeo-Christian ethic that it has all but completely replaced. What was once the majority view, based upon biblically derived principles and understanding, has become the minority view thanks to the mantra spouted across the airwaves and in the classrooms and government corridors of our land.

The Release of the Destruction of Life Devoid of Value

Before proceeding to the next area of complex bioethical issues that have arisen, in part, due to increases in medical technology, this is a good place to insert a brief discussion regarding a pivotal book related to the topic. The entire "quality of life" and "death with dignity" terminology stems from the 1920 volume by Karl Binding and Alfred Hoche entitled *The Release of the Destruction of Life Devoid of Value: Its Measure and Its Form.* The book was written in German, but it was reprinted in English in 1975 by Robert Sassone. The two authors had a heavy dose of the influence of German philosophers of the preceding 140 or so years, including Kant, Hegel and Nietzsche—not to mention the sequiturs that stemmed from the conclusions of natural scientists von Humboldt and Darwin. This book was seminal in the formation of a worldview that served to devalue human life in our modern era and was absolutely foundational in Hitler's Germany, as it became popular in Germany and much of Europe in the decade preceding the rise of Nazism and was thus in the social mind of pre-Nazi Germany. Initially, it was met with shock but, over the space of a decade as the shocking *unthinkable* was discussed and debated in a public forum, the unthinkable moved from *unthinkable* to *thinkable* to *popular.*[109]

A synopsis of the book, located on the website for the *Center for Holocaust & Genocide Studies* at the University of Minnesota, makes a direct connection between the book and "the Nazi policy of extermination."[110] The book is said to have been the source most quoted by the defense at the Nuremberg Trials.

The book has also provided the basis for many discussions on the subject of euthanasia and eugenics

---

[109]http://www.chgs.umn.edu/histories/documentary/hadamar/racism.html, Accessed January 19, 2012
[110] Ibid.

following the Third Reich "with [its] juridical arguments in support of the killing of 'life devoid of value,'" a "cost-benefit analysis regarding psychiatric care and described sick and disabled people as 'people with deficits', 'elements of minor value', 'mentally dead' and 'ballast existences;'" and the strong suggestion of the rightness of "the painless killing of 'incurably' sick persons against their will."[111]

A quick Google search of the name of the book or of the authors will show that this book is cited <u>often</u> in the promotion of "death with dignity" laws around the world. It received its *foundation* in Kantian/Hegelian philosophy, its *testing ground* in Hitler's extermination camps, and is *still* being used and cited (or, at least, obliquely-referenced) as a basis for discussion in legislative sessions and courtrooms across the Western world.[112]

---

[111] Ibid.
[112] Two examples among many can be viewed at the following sites. http://leg.state.nv.us/Session/68th1995/minutes/SJD322.txt - and - http://www.all.org/article/index/id/MjM4Nw. Others can be found easily through in Internet search.

Life Support, Pain Management and Acts that Kill

As stated in Chapter 1, there is a great deal of difference between *allowing someone to die* who would not maintain physical life without "extraordinary means" of intervention and the *performing of an act* that would take a person's life who would not otherwise die without the performance of that act. I suppose I should define some of these terms, as I intend for their meaning to be understood for our purposes here.

Please note, however, that the terms "extraordinary means" or "extraordinary measures" have been used frequently in such bioethical debates—on both sides of the issue—and in various settings, yet without any uniform definition. By *"extraordinary means (measures) of intervention,"* I mean the use of a medical device, system or agent that prolongs the physical life of an individual unnaturally and without which the person would die in the immediate future.

By the term *"performing of an act,"* I mean an intentional action that would *cause* a person to physically die in the immediate future when that person would not die in the immediate future if the action were not performed. Additionally, the term applies to the intentional neglect of a duty (such as feeding, or another basic life necessity) through purposeful inaction with intention of hastening a death. While someone is being given basic life necessities, palliative care, that is comfort-care and pain management, can and should be used to ease suffering as it is needed. This is far different than administering a lethal dose of morphine to a patient—a dose that prematurely stops either respiration or slows their heart rate to the point of making life unsustainable.

At first glance these are simple concepts, but the myriad nuances surrounding such situations can make it quite complex. For example, if the attending physicians state that a loved one is dying and their digestive system has shut down—meaning a feeding tube would simply put materials into their system that could not be utilized, but would rather put undue pressure on the digestive system and cause pain—then perhaps a feeding tube would be inappropriate. If, however, there was reason to believe that feeding (a basic life necessity) would benefit the body and prolong their life, and if there was a chance the patient would come out of their present state, then it appears the measures should be continued.

Some may argue that if the person could not feed themselves, then the feeding tube would constitute "an extraordinary measure" that prolongs life without benefit of any quality of life. This argument is shortsighted. A newborn infant also relies upon means beyond its capabilities to receive needed nutrition. He or she relies upon others for food, shelter and more—without which a baby's death would be certain. Therefore the reliance upon others for basic life needs does not by itself constitute extraordinary measures.

There are many nuances to these end-of-life situations and this book cannot spell out all of them with definitive advice. Yet the principles that should guide us are presented here for your consideration—hopefully before you find yourself facing a crisis situation. When faced with such issues, you may need to stand your ground in the face of opposition. Let biblical principles be your guide.

The line between allowing a person to die and the performance of an act to hasten the death of an individual has been blurred greatly in the recent decades since Roe v. Wade. In a Senate Committee on Judiciary, State of Nevada, March 22, 1995 an interesting discussion was recorded relative to Senate Bill SB 234 that was designed to prohibit the act of assisting suicide. In the discussion, one representative of Nevada Concerned Citizens, Ms. Lucille Lusk, offered an articulate view representing a traditional Judeo-Christian stance on the sanctity of human life. She stated, "Nearly everyone supports the right of individuals to choose their own medical care, including the refusal or removal from artificial means of life support." She went on to state that the Senate bill in question was an attempt "to prevent the crossing to an affirmative act that prematurely causes the death of a person who would not have otherwise died of natural causes at that time," and to "prevent the movement toward the unwanted assisted suicide of elderly persons."

Her point was all but ridiculed openly by the Chair of the Senate Committee, Mark A. James (R), who proceeded to attempt persuasive argument in favor of assisted suicide.[113]

The discussion was not only interesting, but it also pointed out the earlier-mentioned statement by theology professor David VanDrunen in his timely book on

---

[113] http://leg.state.nv.us/Session/68th1995/minutes/SJD322.txt

120

bioethics: "Many bioethical decisions simply do not have one absolutely binding right or wrong answer."[114]

Physician-assisted suicide (euthanasia), once illegal throughout the United States, is not only becoming legal in multiple states—societal attitudes regarding its morality are also shifting dramatically in the face of a concerted effort to change our culture. In 2001, 49% of those polled by the Gallup organization considered doctor-assisted suicide to be morally acceptable.

In 2015 that number shifted to a majority of 56%. Only 37% stated that they felt it to be "morally wrong."[115] In my own state of California, a bill was passed last year (2015) making physician-assisted suicide legal. The bill was signed into law October 15, 2015. Oregon's law, the *Oregon Death With Dignity Act*, passed in 1994; and, after several challenges, was finally upheld by the U.S. Supreme Court in 2006 in *Gonzales v. Oregon*.[116]

In that SCOTUS decision, Justices Scalia, Roberts and Thomas dissented in the 6-3 vote. With Justice Scalia's

---

[114] VanDrunen, p.16
[115] http://www.gallup.com/poll/183413/americans-continue-shift-left-key-moral-issues.aspx, accessed October 31, 2016
[116] https://www.law.cornell.edu/supct/html/04-623.ZS.html, Accessed October 31, 2016

position awaiting replacement at the time of this writing due to his recent death, with Justice Thomas likely to be replaced in the next presidency (Donald Trump was just elected as I write), and along with the lack of predictability of the actions of Supreme Court appointments, it is looking more likely that legislative efforts now working through other states, if they pass, would be upheld. As the years pass and the inevitable slide toward a humanistic worldview takes a greater foothold in our society, it is all but certain this decay will be reflected in the Supreme Court.

The most recent state to adopt a similar measure was Colorado on their November 2016 ballot initiative, Proposition 106, which allows for "medical aid in dying." This was put on the voter ballots and it passed easily with nearly 65% of the votes cast in favor of the measure. According to a New York Times report about the measure, "the proposition calls for allowing terminally ill patients to take their own lives using medication prescribed by a doctor."[117] Of course, the doctor would need to prescribe

---

[117] http://www.nytimes.com/elections/results/colorado-ballot-measure-106-medical-aid-in-dying, Accessed November 23, 2016.

the "medication"—thus presenting a potential ethical dilemma for the attending physician as well.

A stunning article in *Christianity Today* relayed the results of a recent survey conducted by Nashville-based LifeWay Research.[118] Participants were asked to indicate whether they agreed or disagreed with certain statements regarding physician-assisted suicide.

The survey of 1,000 Americans was conducted from September 27 through October 1, 2016 and asked participants to self-identify as either holding "evangelical beliefs" or not.[119] A number of other subgroups were identified in the survey including gender, region, age, frequency of religious service attendance and more. As we shall see, the study paints a very telling and very disturbing picture of a shifting mindset in our culture—even among those calling themselves evangelicals, a group that largely claims to take the Bible literally.

118

http://www.christianitytoday.com/gleanings/2016/december/opposition -to-assisted-suicide-dies-out-lifeway.html, Accessed December 6, 2016
[119] http://lifewayresearch.com/2016/12/06/most-americans-say-assisted-suicide-is-morally-acceptable/, Accessed December 13, 2016. The survey has a 95% statistical confidence with a margin of error of ±3.1%. Margins of error are higher in subgroups.

Complex Bioethical Issues

Let's look at the responses comparing all Americans with the subgroup identifying as holding evangelical beliefs:

Statement	Response	
-	**All Americans**	**Those with Evangelical Beliefs**
"When a person is facing a painful terminal disease, it is morally acceptable to ask for a physician's aid in taking his or her own life."	67% agree	38% agree
"Physicians should be allowed to assist terminally ill patients in ending their lives."	69% agree	42% agree

It is troubling that those who self-identified as holding evangelical beliefs agreed with these statements in large percentages. There is an increasingly secular viewpoint on this issue even among so-called evangelicals. Where would these numbers stand among self-identified Apostolics? Pastors, do you know how members of your congregation view these issues? Have you taken the time to teach them what the Scriptures say regarding the inherent sanctity of human life?

Christians need to understand that the mere fact that something is *legal* does not make that same something *moral*. Voices of pastors need to be lifted to counter the prevailing culture. Sound biblical teaching regarding the centuries-long-held understanding of the sanctity of human life is *critical* at the hour in which we live. We cannot afford to wait until personal crises arise in which decisions must be made under duress—decisions that are of extreme moral consequence.

The voices of the "death with dignity" advocates are smooth and convincing to those watching their loved ones suffer with disease. "After all, we consider it 'humane' to euthanize a dog with cancer but immoral to euthanize our father with cancer." It sure sounds convincing when you remove God's perspective from view, yet we can only get a proper perspective from the Word of God—and not from emotionally-charged rhetoric. "Let God be true, but every man a liar" (Romans 3:4).

Chapter Seven

Where Do We Go From Here?

"It was a bright cold day in April, and the clocks were striking thirteen."

George Orwell, 1949
Opening line of Nineteen Eighty-Four

"Any man's death diminishes me, because I am involved in mankind; and therefore, never send to know for whom the bell tolls; It tolls for thee."

John Donne, 1624
Devotions Upon Emergent Occasions
Meditation XVII

I am convinced that we are in the closing days of time, and that the assault on our Bible-based values will only continue to escalate. Because of the many medical advances that have been and are being made, more and more complex bioethical questions relative to the sanctity of life will be faced by our parishioners as they confront their personal issues of life and death.

For this reason, it is imperative that pastors and teachers become "engaged in"—as opposed to "removed from"—the necessary teaching of the biblical principles of the uniqueness, preciousness, and sanctity of human life so that these principles become part of our nature as we grapple with the surrounding culture.

It is imperative that these principles become engrafted into the makeup and thinking of the ministry and our congregants—for the challenges presented in this book are challenges each of us will face at some time in our lives. We must prepare ourselves and our congregations, through study and proper preaching and teaching, to know how we will face the monumental events that are our inescapable lot. Christians working in the healthcare community need to become and remain aware of the humanistic mindset that is being promoted with increasing frequency within their industry through trade periodicals, medical schools, blogs, and in some continuing education courses—and stand fast against that encroaching mindset even when it is promoted among your peers.

In 2009, the United States Conference of Catholic Bishops published the fifth edition of *Ethical and Religious Directives for Catholic Health Care Services.*[120] Parts four and five of the document deal, respectively, with issues of care involving the beginning of life and the seriously ill and dying. This document consistently portrays a conservative stand on the absolute sanctity of human life. It acknowledges that "the Catholic health care ministry witnesses to the sanctity of life 'from the moment of conception until death.'"[121] The same document also states, "...two extremes are avoided: on the one hand, an insistence on useless or burdensome technology even when a patient may legitimately wish to forgo it and, on the other hand, the withdrawal of technology with the intention of causing death." It covers many issues such as nutrition and hydration to the seriously ill and dying in a way that largely

---

[120] http://www.ncbcenter.org/document.doc?id=147, Accessed March 3, 2012
[121] http://www.ncbcenter.org/document.doc?id=147, p.23

lies within the bounds of scriptural principles regarding the intrinsic sanctity of human life.

In February 2012, national news reverberated with the story of the ObamaCare mandate that all hospital institutions comply with the law that requires all healthcare providers, including Catholic and other faith-based providers, to provide free contraception (paid through employers' health insurance), including abortifacients.[122,123] In an interview I had with a representative of Dignity Health (formerly Catholic Healthcare West) in early 2012, I was told "the bishops have said that is one law they are going to ignore." He also suggested there was serious pressure from the [Obama] administration, and that he saw "some signs that they [were] cracking."[124] Who knows how long it will be before, under the leadership of left-leaning Pope Francis, they capitulate completely to the mantra, and then join it.

Such conflicts are growing both in intensity and frequency, and I am afraid they portend the future in our

---

[122] A substance that induces abortion.
[123] http://www.nationalreview.com/articles/290986/hhs-mandate-why-deroy-murdock, Accessed March 3, 2012
[124] Personal interview held February 10, 2012—name of interviewee withheld.

contention for biblical righteousness in the various life issues surrounding medical ethics and the absolute sanctity of human life from the moment of conception. Things are bound to get worse; indeed, "evil men and seducers shall wax worse and worse, deceiving, and being deceived."[125] We need to sound a clarion call and stand well above the moral baseness of our society that calls darkness light and light darkness.[126]

I call upon pastors, teachers, and counselors to teach these principles, and for them and Christian medical professionals to become and stay aware of the social trends relative to the humanistic "culture of death" in our society, and to assist those who depend on them for guidance—using the Scriptures as their guide.

---

[125] II Timothy 3:13
[126] Isaiah 5:20

Glossary of Terms

a priori - that which is existing in the mind prior to and independent of experience; not based on study or prior examination.

abortifacient - a drug or device used to cause abortion.

abortion - the removal of an embryo or fetus from the uterus in order to end a pregnancy or a chemically induced means of causing the uterus to expel the fetus such as the use of "the morning after pill."

abortion-on-demand - an abortion performed on a woman solely at her own request regardless of any underlying reason.

amniocentesis - a surgical procedure for obtaining a sample of amniotic fluid from the amniotic sac in the uterus of a pregnant woman; used in diagnosing certain genetic defects such as Down syndrome, or possible obstetric complications.

biblical absolutes - truths that are inviolable/immutable in that they are derived directly from the Scriptures.

bioethics - a field of study concerned with the ethics and philosophical implications of certain biological and medical procedures, technologies, and treatments, as organ transplants, genetic engineering, and care of the terminally ill. Subsets include medical bioethics and medical ethics.

blastocyst - the modified blastula that is characteristic of placental mammals (including humans). It has an outer layer, known as a trophoblast, which participates in the development of the placenta. The inner layer of cells develops into the embryo.

culture of death - a term coined by Pope John Paul II in his 1995 *Evangelium Vitae* used to refer to the spread of a culture accepting of abortion, euthanasia The term has been used in a plethora of anti-abortion/anti-euthanasia literature.

death with dignity - a philosophical approach in which a patient choses the time and means of ending their life when medicaments are not likely to be effective in either curing a condition or increasing the quality of life. It stems from a secular humanistic construct.

Declaration of Geneva - a declaration adopted in September 1948 by the General Assembly of the World Medical Association and closely modeled on the Hippocratic Oath. It became widely used as the graduation oath many medical schools.

DNA - deoxyribonucleic acid: an extremely long macromolecule that is the main component of chromosomes and is the material that transfers genetic characteristics in all life forms.

ectopic pregnancy – a pregnancy in which the embryo becomes implanted somewhere other than in the uterus—most often in the fallopian tubes that connect the ovaries to the uterus. This often presents as an emergency situation wherein an expectant mother's life could be placed in peril.

euthanasia - a euphemism for the act of putting to death painlessly or allowing to die, as by withholding medical measures, food or oxygen, a person suffering from an incurable, especially a painful, disease or condition.

Gallup - an American research-based, global performance-management consulting company known for its public opinion polls.

Hippocratic Oath - An oath of ethical professional behavior sworn by new physicians and attributed to Hippocrates. This oath served as the basis for the *Declaration of Geneva* and subsequent oaths taken by new physicians.

human autonomy - the secular humanistic belief that man is the final arbiter of what is truth and what is not, and the idea that man's morality and ultimate destiny are derived from his own ability to reason and not from any deity.

humanism (secular humanism) - while there are many divergent forms of humanism, the term generally refers to a secular, atheistic (or at least agnostic) view that deifies man and dethrones God as the final arbiter of what is true. It makes human reasoning the yardstick for determining what is ethical, moral and worthwhile.

Humanist Manifesto - Humanist Manifestos I, II and III were published in 1933, 1973 and 2003, respectively. They codify the generally agreed upon tenets of humanistic thought in the 20th and early 21st centuries. The term Humanist Manifesto may refer to any of these three documents, or to all of them collectively.

in utero - within the uterus.

in vitro fertilization - a technique by which a human ovum is fertilized by sperm outside the body, with the resulting embryo later implanted in the uterus for gestation (test tube baby).

infanticide - the killing of newborn infants. Modern (20th and 21st century) Western medical ethics literature is replete with so-called justifications for infanticide in the case of birth defects wherein the infant is determined by others to have a life that is "devoid of value."

infertility - the persistent inability to achieve conception and produce an offspring without the aid of medical intervention such as the use of in vitro fertilization or the use of a surrogate donor of sperm and/or ova or the use of a surrogate mother to carry a fetus to birth.

ObamaCare (Obamacare) - the Patient Protection and Affordable Care Act (PPACA), commonly called the Affordable Care Act (ACA) or Obamacare, is a United States federal statute enacted by President Barack Obama on March 23, 2010.

palliative care – also referred to as palliative measures, care that focuses on improving life and providing comfort to people of all ages with serious, chronic, and life-threatening illnesses. It often refers to pain management and other comfort care measures for those facing terminal illnesses or conditions.

persistent vegetative state (PVS) - a condition of unresponsiveness to mental and physical stimuli and with no sign of higher brain function.

pluripotent - (of a cell) capable of developing into any type of cell or tissue except those that form a placenta or embryo.

prima facie - at first appearance; at first view, before investigation. Used in this book as meaning: What is espoused and repeated without opposition will become accepted as fact by those that hear it.

pro-choice - having the view of supporting or advocating the supposed right to an abortion. It is based upon two related false premises: 1. that a woman has a right to choose what she does with her own body, and 2. the fetus within a woman is part of her own body and not another human being.

proleptically - the representation of something in the future as if it already existed or had occurred.

Roe v. Wade - the landmark 1973 Supreme Court decision that opened the door for the legalization of abortion across the United States in certain circumstances. This decision paved the way to subsequent decisions allowing for abortion-on-demand.

SCOTUS - Supreme Court of the United States

situational ethics - the belief that ethical decisions should follow flexible guidelines rather than absolute rules (such as biblical absolutes), and be taken on a case by case basis. It is a fixed belief of secular humanists that "ethics is autonomous and situational needing no theological or ideological sanction."

Glossary of Terms

stem cell - an unspecialized cell found in fetuses, embryos, and some adult body tissues with the potential to develop into specialized cells. Stem cells from fetuses or embryos can develop into any type of differentiated cells (see *pluripotent*), while those found in mature tissues develop only into specific cells. Stem cells can potentially be used to replace tissue damaged or destroyed by disease or injury. The most promising results have been attributed to adult stem cell research rather than embryonic stem cell research.

zygote - the cell formed by the union of two gametes (sperm and egg), especially a fertilized ovum before cleavage.

zygotic - pertaining to a zygote. Twins that are monozygotic come from a single zygote and are known as "identical twins" whereas twins that are dizygotic come from two separate zygotes and are known as "fraternal twins."

Index

Index

141

- Notes -

- Notes -

- Notes -

- Notes –

Made in the USA
Middletown, DE
27 August 2018